DYNASTY

DYNASTY

THE RISE AND FALL OF THE
GREATEST TEAMS IN NBA HISTORY

AGU IBAÑEZ-BALDOR

NEW DEGREE PRESS

COPYRIGHT © 2020 AGU IBAÑEZ-BALDOR

DYNASTY

The Rise and Fall of the Greatest Teams in NBA History

ISBN   978-1-64137-901-4   *Paperback*

          978-1-64137-623-5   *Kindle Ebook*

          978-1-64137-625-9   *Ebook*

CONTENTS

ACKNOWLEDGMENTS

———

First and foremost, I would like to thank my family for encouraging me to do this in the first place and for picking me up whenever I was down on myself. I never would have been able to do anything (let alone write this book) without you.

Thanks to all my college friends for still being friends with me despite me being a trolly dumbass for most of our exploits. Shout-out to Hansen for reading my stuff even before there was a confirmation that the thing would get published. Shout-out to Dante for reading chapters and giving me feedback within an hour every single time. Also, shout-out to the Michigan Street 8 for boolin' with me through the good and the bad (I love you all so fuckin' much).

Shout-out to David O'Keefe and his family for being probably the most enthusiastic people during the preorder campaign. Your energy and mass-spread of my posts helped in more ways than just monetary.

Shout-out to Liam McMahon for always answering my absurd sports texts and being supportive of my career aspirations from the very start. Also, for never hesitating to let me know when I am being a little much—I need that sometimes.

Shout-out to the Adams family, the Bolich's, the Lockhart's, the Baudhuin's, the Murphy's, and Alysa Schulte for just POURING money into my preorder campaign. You guys accounted for a sixth of the donations alone, and that is crazy. Thank you for believing in me enough to pay one hundred dollars plus for a couple paperback books (and perks).

I would love to give a massive shout-out to New Degree Press, Brian Bies, Linda Berardelli, and anyone else who put up with my antics and is actually allowing me to publish a book. Shout-out especially to Eric Koester; I likely never would have written a book in my life had you not messaged me on LinkedIn in August of 2019. Thank you so much for what you do in this class and your pure intentions behind it.

Lastly, I would like to thank anyone and everyone that contributed to the completion of this book; you guys are my faves:

Katherine Adams	Matt Delage
Martina Ibañez-Baldor	John Donovan
Maria J. Baldor	Dante Gonzalez
Sam Shefrin	Jeff David
Eric Koester	Chris Doukas
Connor McColl	Pol Vandevelde
Nikolina Kosanovic	Ralph Ibañez
Harry Bolich	Rodrigo Ibañez

Wayne Ferguson
Javier Ibañez-Baldor
Joan Randolph
Mason Peressini
Liam McMahon
Dan Scallon
Spencer Michaelis
Tanner Wallenkamp
Hannah Mauch
Cheyanne Hagan
Meghan Ryan
Alex Amaya
Callahan Rohde
Brooke M Price
John Murphy
Maria Piotrowski
Jon Fisher
Heather O'Keeffe
Jessica Bango
Paul O'Keeffe
Robert Hermann
Patrick Baudhuin
Scott Stangel
Anusha Das
David Kubicek
Jackson Telderer
Madeline Glawe
Mary Tyler Curtis
Tracy S Lockhart
Denny Moyer
Sean Murphy
Molly Rockwood

Sandy Gleason
Joe Albrecht
Randall Tranowski
Konner Szohr
Jean E. Carter
Richard C Taylor
Nicole Sygieda
Samantha Hermsen
Tomas Ohannessian
Thomas Borin
Anthony Peressini
Mariana Ibañez-Baldor
Brendan Blaney
Nicholas Hansen
Keith and Cecilia Adams
Alexandra Andringa
David O'Keeffe
Joseph Romfoe
Michelle Guyant-Holloway
Logan Aguilar
Daniel Abalos
Tim Foley
Joseph Paetsch
Zachary Steven
Keara Clacko
Nick Reddy
Richie Dehnel
Philip Olsen
Alysa Schulte
Gail Bonofiglio
Tom Murphy
Dan O'Keeffe

Emily Quinnett
Laura Sienkiewicz
Meri White
Sarrah Oliver
Tami Nelsen
Sarah Kimmel
Dominic Maretti
Laerte Venturi
Michael Dahlquist
Luke Brucker
Sherrill Knezel

Nicole deGuzman
Monica Speranza
Bo Chen
David Twetten
Drew Foren
Maddy Rockhold
Mo Coffey
Ericka Tucker
Lauren Minette
Paige Hunt

INTRODUCTION

Building a championship team usually can't be rushed, and building a dynasty requires otherworldly patience. There have been only four National Basketball Association (NBA) teams to win three or more championships in a row, and the last time it happened was nearly two decades ago. What does it take to not only achieve success, but maintain it?

Sometimes all it takes is one generational player like LeBron James. While it may not take as much to win a championship with him, the teams around him have had quick expiration dates. Teams like the '80s Bulls, the early 2000s Lakers, and the late 2010s Golden State Warriors (the most recent dynasty) achieved that championship success and maintained it for several years. Most people will point to the fact that those teams had Michael Jordan, Kobe Bryant, and Stephen Curry as the reason for this extended success. The truth is that they are a huge part of that success, but they are not the full reason. Those teams had brilliant front offices that made hard decisions to build the perfect teams around those respective superstars.

TAKE FOR INSTANCE THE NEW JERSEY/BROOKLYN NETS

On May 11, 2010, Mikhail Prokhorov became the majority owner of the New Jersey Nets. With a new owner came new expectations. He wanted to contend for a title immediately and would pay any price to get there. In that spirit, the Nets made three massive trades over the span of a couple years. On February 11, 2011, the Nets traded for star point guard Deron Williams. In return, they sent the Utah Jazz:

- Power forward Derrick Favors and point guard Devin Harris
- An unprotected 2011 first-round pick and a 2013 unprotected first-round pick

The team did not make the playoffs that following season or the season after. In 2012, the team moved back to New York and became the Brooklyn Nets.

> **Exposition Time!**
> The Nets were originally the New Jersey Americans in the American Basketball Association (ABA), then moved and became the New York Nets from 1968 to 1976, returned to New Jersey when they merged with the NBA and became the New Jersey Nets until 2012.

With a new city, new fans, and a new arena, there was even more pressure to contend quickly. The Nets made another trade to relieve the pressure. On July 11, 2012, the Nets

traded to the Atlanta Hawks in return for star forward
Joe Johnson:

- Point guard Jordan Farmar, shooting guard Anthony
  Morrow, forward DeShawn Stevenson, and centers Jordan Williams and Johan Petro
- An unprotected 2013 first-round pick and an unprotected
  2017 second-round pick

The team made the playoffs for the first time in five seasons.
They lost to the Chicago Bulls in seven games. Prokhorov
and the front office were not satisfied. They made one more
Godfather trade in an attempt to buy a championship and
possibly a dynasty. They traded:

- Power forward Kris Humphries (of Kardashian fame),
  small forwards Kris Joseph and Gerald Wallace, and
  shooting guards Keith Bogans and MarShon Brooks
- Unprotected first-round picks in 2014, 2016, 2017, and 2018
  with a pick swap available in 2017 as well

In return, they got future Hall of Famers Kevin Garnett and
Paul Pierce from the Boston Celtics. They also received Jason
Terry, D.J. White, and 2017 first and second-round picks.
With Garnett, Pierce, Williams, and Johnson paired with
the up-and-coming Brook Lopez, the Nets had compiled a
starting lineup that had more than five All-NBA appearances, more than ten All-Defense appearances, and more
than twenty All-Star appearances. Garnett and Pierce were
two of the best players on the championship Celtics team
just a few years back. The issue was that at the start of the
2013–14 season, only Williams and Lopez were under thirty,

and Williams was twenty-nine. Garnett, Pierce, and Johnson were all at the tail end of their careers, let alone their primes. Despite some early success with this newly assembled team, the consequences of these moves would come about soon.

The Nets made the playoffs and won a playoff series that year, their first in six seasons. They lost in the second round. After the season, Paul Pierce left in free agency. Halfway through 2014–15, the Nets traded Garnett to the Timberwolves in exchange for Thaddeus Young. The team made the playoffs but lost in the first round to Atlanta (the team that had traded them Joe Johnson). Brooklyn waived both Deron Williams and Joe Johnson in the following season. They were stuck at the bottom of the NBA with no real picks to improve until the late 2010s. They have yet to win a playoff series since 2013–14.

In the end, the Nets traded thirteen players and ten unprotected draft picks in return for three playoff appearances, with just one series win to show for it. The Celtics, since 2013–14, have won five playoff series and have built one of the best young cores in the league, almost entirely with the picks they received from Brooklyn.

This here is a lesson.

DYNASTY takes a hard look at how each dynasty in NBA history was constructed and maintained, and how they eventually fell. For the purposes of this book, a dynasty is defined as a team that won three or more championships in a five-year period. Several teams got close to this, making three or four Finals in a five-year period but not winning three or more, and so they did not make the cut. If one of those teams happens to be one of your favorite teams, please tweet me @aguibanezbaldor with insults and threats that would make Ari Aster blush.

Did one team use drafting while another used free agency, and another used trades? Was it a combination of the three? How much did the coaching and system matter? What were the differences in the decisions made to have an impact both now and later, not just one or the other? After we have answered those questions and more, I want to see whether the contenders of today's NBA are mirroring any of these decisions. Are any of the on-the-cusp teams making the strides to get there? Are the rebuilding teams focused on future success with dynasties in mind?

I'm a basketball nerd who's watched for most of his twenty-two-year-old life and reads and listens to anything NBA-related that I can get my hands on. I'm not going to pretend like these findings are definitive or that NBA teams should use this book as a guide for building a dynasty. I want to point out parallels between the greatest teams in NBA history and teams today.

There's a solid chance that my findings are inconclusive and flat-out wrong. Of course, if I am right about even the most minuscule detail, I will be taking full credit and crowning myself as Basketball's Hispanic Jesus (sorry Shea). I will also be expecting calls from Mark Cuban and Pat Riley with congratulations on my success and questions about my basketball future. (Hey, if either of you are reading this, I'm totally kidding. Unless you think this book is smart and indicative of someone who can succeed in your world. In that case, I'm deadly serious.)

This book is split into three parts. The "Respect Your Elders" section covers the first two dynasties in NBA history: the Minneapolis Lakers and the Bill Russell-led Boston Celtics. The "Modern Era" section covers every dynasty from the '80s up to the present in 2020. That era includes teams like the Michael Jordan Bulls, the immortal San Antonio Spurs, and the most recent NBA dynasty: the Golden State Warriors (GSW). I also will be introducing an eight-category formula I developed that will run through each team in the "Modern Era" to give them a "Dynasty Score." I'll give more details on the formula itself once we get there. Finally, we have the "Bonus Fun" chapters. These are chapters I wrote on the Larry Bird Celtics, LeBron's eight straight Finals run, and the "Dynasty That Never Was." These teams didn't make the cut the way I defined a dynasty but warranted talking about either because they were super close, they were very interesting cases, or just because I'm afraid of certain national writers. Please check out these chapters before going through with the threats mentioned previously.

Through this analysis of dynasties, I'm hoping to come to a closer understanding of the mystic, methodology, and magic (check out that alliteration, baby!) of building a team for the ages. Whether you're a member of Laker nation, a Bronstan, or a fan of the twenty-nine other teams in the NBA (I've heard they exist, but ESPN has led me to believe other things), you're going to love this book. Unless you don't. In which case... *shrug*

Let's get into it.

CHAPTER 1:

THE FIRST DYNASTY

——

No conversation about NBA dynasties would be complete without mentioning the Minneapolis Lakers, the first NBA dynasty.

While the Los Angeles Lakers are one of the most successful and popular sports organizations in history, the team actually began in Detroit (stay with me here). In 1947, an ownership group in Minnesota bought the recently disbanded Detroit Gems for $15,000 (roughly $170,000 today).[1] They moved the team to Minneapolis and renamed the team to reflect the "Land of 10,000 Lakes." The Lakers would play their first season as a team in the National Basketball League (NBL), winning the title in 1948. After that season, the NBL merged with the Basketball Association of America (BAA), creating the NBA that would eventually evolve into the league we know and love today.[2]

---

1   Jerry Crowe, "Minneapolis Sportswriter Helped Raise the Lakers," *Los Angeles Times*, April 27, 2009.
2   "Lakers Season Capsules," Lakers History, National Basketball Association, accessed May 10, 2020.

ROSTER

The Minneapolis Lakers boasted four future Hall of Famers on their roster; two of them—Jim Pollard and George Mikan—were inherited with the Detroit purchase. At point/shooting guard, they started Slater Martin, a defensive-minded player who was listed at just 5'10". A number of players would fill the other guard spot for the Lakers throughout the dynasty run. Hall of Famer Jim Pollard manned the small forward position for the team. He was nicknamed "the Kangaroo Kid" for his athletic exploits. The team acquired Vern Mikkelsen after his college career in Minnesota following the 1949 offseason. At 6'7", Mikkelsen's natural position (at that time) was center. However, Head Coach John Kundla convinced him to make the move to forward and he became one of the first (if not the first) "power" forwards in basketball. True to the name, Mikkelsen was a tenacious defender and rebounder. In addition to being a Hall of Famer, Mikkelsen was an iron man, playing in 699 out of 704 games in his career (he also fouled out an NBA record 127 times in his career; congrats).

The greatest player from this team and era in basketball, however, was George Mikan. At 6'10", Mikan was the first great center in Lakers history. He also happened to be the NBA's first superstar. Mikan was sponsored by Beech-Nut Gum and was seen on the back of *LIFE* magazine in beer ads, some of the first-ever athletic sponsorships. He would arrive to cities a day earlier than the rest of the team to do interviews promoting the games.[3] Leading the league in scoring for

---

3   "Legends Profile: George Mikan," NBA History, Turner Sports & Entertainment Digital Network, accessed May 10, 2020.

the first three years of his career, Mikan would have been named the Most Valuable Player (MVP) all three years, but the NBA did not introduce the award until 1955. The league introduced goaltending in direct response to his dominance on the defensive end.

Contrary to popular belief, the NBA actually first widened the lane from six to twelve feet due to Mikan's control of the paint (the "Mikan Rule"). His dominance in the paint forced the NBA to widen it so other players could have a chance. They widened it even more due to Wilt Chamberlain's dominance later on.[4] Wilt had tremendous respect for George Mikan, stating:

"He showed the world that a big man could be an athlete."[5]

Mikan retired after the 1954 season and became a lawyer (he had already passed the Bar prior to his basketball career). Later on, he would become the first commissioner of the ABA.[6]

The team was led by Head Coach John Kundla. Kundla had served in World War II and was known for his levelheadedness and respect for his players. Not only is he a Hall of Famer, Kundla was named one of the ten best coaches in NBA history in 1996. In direct contrast to the fiery sergeants

4   "Lakers Season Capsules," Lakers History, National Basketball Association, accessed May 10, 2020.

5   Michael Schumacher, *Mr. Basketball: George Mikan, the Minneapolis Lakers, and the Birth of the NBA* (New York: Bloomsbury, 2007), 33.

6   Joe Moore and Tim Bontemps, "The ABA Is Long Gone, but it Remains the Soul of the NBA," *The Washington Post*, May 31, 2017.

who coached most of the teams at the time, Kundla preached "praise loudly and blame softly." While he did fall victim to the classic "he inherited a good team" narrative, much of the team's psychological success has been attributed to him. His approach helped maintain the egos of several superstars on his team. Former player Whitey Skoog said the following about Kundla's coaching style:

"He was never negative about a player's mistakes. He worked to find a way for the player to improve. He never criticized a player in the press and gave the players the credit for the Lakers' success."[7]

After his NBA coaching career, Kundla became the head coach at the University of Minnesota. Along with his success there, he is known for being the first Minnesota coach to offer scholarships to African American players.[8]

DYNASTY

The Minneapolis Lakers won five titles in six years (1949–54). They also won the championship in 1948 when they were still part of the NBL. Here's a quick rundown of their titles in the NBA:

1949: Lakers beat Chicago Stags 2–0 in the first round. Lakers beat Rochester Royals 2–0 in the second round. Lakers beat

---

7   Joel Ripper, "John Kundla, Former Minneapolis Lakers Coach and Basketball Hall of Famer, Dies at 101," *Star Tribune*, July 24, 2017.

8   Ibid.

Washington Capitals 4–2 to win the championship. Mikan leads playoffs in points and Pollard leads in assists.

- **1950:** Lakers beat Stags 2–0 in the first round. Lakers beat Fort Wayne Pistons 2–0 in the second round. Lakers beat Anderson Packers 2–0 to advance to the Finals. Lakers beat Syracuse Nationals 4–2 to win the title. Mikan and Pollard again lead the playoffs in points and assists, respectively.
- **1951:** Lakers lose 1–3 in the second round to the Rochester Royals, the eventual champions of that season.
- **1952:** Lakers beat Indianapolis Olympians 2–0 in the first round. Lakers beat Rochester (exacting revenge) 3–1 in the second round. Lakers beat New York Knicks 4–3 in the Finals. Mikan leads the playoffs in both points and rebounds.
- **1953:** Lakers sweep Olympians in the first round. Lakers beat Fort Wayne 3–2 to go to the Finals. Lakers beat Knicks 4–1 to secure another title. Mikan again scores the most points and secures the most rebounds in the playoffs.
- **1954:** Lakers go 3–0 in the Round Robin first round (the NBA basically changed the playoff format every year in the 50s. Just accept the confusion like I did). Lakers beat Royals 2–1 in the Western Division Finals. Lakers beat Nationals 4–3 in the Finals. Mikan (as you may have assumed) averages the most points and rebounds in the playoffs. Slater Martin ties for the most assists in the playoffs.

The only year the Lakers did not win was in 1951, when Mikan broke his ankle toward the end of the campaign. They still made it to the Conference Finals that year, but no further.

After that season, the NBA widened the lane in an attempt to slow down Mikan's (and the Lakers') dominance. It didn't work. He finished second in scoring and the Lakers won their third championship in four years. They would win two more after that (becoming the first NBA team to three-peat), and Mikan would retire after the 1953–54 season. Two years later, Pollard retired, leaving the Lakers roster a shell of its former self.

Three seasons of mediocre play and one last place finish later, the team drafted Elgin Baylor first overall and the Lakers would soon become a dangerous team yet again. Attendance dwindled heavily after Mikan's retirement, and the financial struggles that came with it forced a change. After the 1960 season, the Lakers moved to Los Angeles (keeping the name) and became the NBA's first West Coast team.[9]

BONUS FUN FACT:

During the 1955–56 season, Sid Hartman (the man who brought the Lakers to Minneapolis and made nearly all their personnel decisions) agreed to a deal with Red Auerbach and the Boston Celtics to send Vern Mikkelsen to them in exchange for three players. The reasoning behind this deal was that the Lakers weren't competing after the Mikan and Pollard retirements and Hartman wanted to tank for the first overall pick. The Lakers ended up pulling away from this deal partly because their play-by-play

---

9   "Lakers Season Capsules," Lakers History, National Basketball Association, accessed May 10, 2020.

broadcaster was so close to Mikkelsen. The Boston Celtics ended up using the draft pick they would have sent to Los Angeles to trade for the second overall pick and took Bill Russell, which jump started the next dynasty in the NBA (stay tuned).

FINAL THOUGHTS:

The formula I mentioned in the Introduction cannot be applied to the Minneapolis Lakers (or the next team for that matter). A number of the metrics used for the formula aren't available for this time period in the NBA, and I would have to skew the formula to the point where it isn't applicable to the modern teams to apply it to these two teams. So, we're going to view the first two dynasties in the NBA more as lessons than blueprints.

We can take away incredibly valuable things from this team— John Kundla's coaching in particular. He was not afraid to change the way the game was played at the time, including moving Mikkelsen to power forward. This is a theme you will see as we examine other dynasties with brilliant coaches. John Kundla managed the personalities on his team perfectly. George Mikan, Jim Pollard, and Vern Mikkelsen all retired as members of the Lakers and Kundla played a massive part in keeping that core together. Slater Martin only left after the Lakers became a losing team. This iteration of the Lakers set the standard for what would become one of the best organizations in NBA history with a seemingly never-ending list of all-time big men.

The Minneapolis Lakers are remembered as the first NBA dynasty, and Mikan as the first great NBA big man. They deserve those titles and more, but they were far from the last.

CHAPTER 2:

DOMINANCE PERSONIFIED

———

We heard you like dominance, so we put dominance in your dynasty so that your dynasty dominated. If you're too young for that joke, I tried to do it with the Tyler the Creator meme ("so you just gonna bring me a birthday gift to my birthday party…"), but it didn't work. If you don't understand either of those references, congrats! I just wasted three sentences of your life.

All incredibly solid jokes and references aside, the Boston Celtics dominated the league in the late '50s and all the '60s in a way that we haven't seen since. They won ELEVEN titles in thirteen seasons. No team, besides the Lakers, has more than six total titles! How did the Boston Celtics build a team with the most wins in league history? It all began with their coach selection.

BUILDING A DYNASTY

The Celtics were a fledgling team when the league began—a fun, but unsuccessful team. In 1950, Boston finished last in the league. Walter Brown (the team's owner at the time) decided to make a change at coach. An informal advisory board, hired due to Brown's lack of basketball knowledge, decided that Red Auerbach was the best man for the job. Up to that point, Auerbach was a somewhat successful NBA coach, but he had not won anything of significance. In the beginning, Auerbach wanted to do everything by himself. He had no assistant coaches, ran all the practices, and did all of the scouting (on other teams and college prospects) on his own. He would soon gain a reputation for having an eye for talent.

Bob Cousy was perhaps the greatest college player the year that Auerbach was hired for the Celtics. What was better, is that he played for Holy Cross, which was right in Massachusetts. Despite this, Auerbach refused to draft him. He thought Cousy was "too flashy" for his preferred "team basketball" style:

"We need a big man," Auerbach said at the time. "Little men are a dime a dozen. I'm supposed to win, not go after local yokels."[10]

Instead, Auerbach would select Chuck Cooper and become the first franchise to draft an African American player.[11]

---

10 Larry Schwartz, "Celtics Tried to Pass on Ultimate Passer," *ESPN*, accessed May 10, 2020.

11 Lisette Hilton, "Auerbach's Celtics Played as a Team," *ESPN*, accessed May 10, 2020.

Cousy, in the meantime, was drafted by the Tri-City Black-hawks. Soon after, the Blackhawks would trade him to the Chicago Stags, a team that folded before the 1950–1951 season. Three players from the Stags were up for grabs, and their names were put into a hat. Owners of the Celtics, Knicks, and Philadelphia Warriors gathered in a hotel room to draw names. The Celtics drew Cousy.[12] Despite Auerbach's initial concerns, it ended up working out for them. Cousy may have been flashy, but it was in a way that helped the team. He was electric on the fast break and led the league in assists eight times. He hit double digits in both All-Star games and First Team All-NBA selections. He was a bona fide Hall of Famer and one of several that Auerbach coached.

Jumping to the 1956 draft, Auerbach had his eye on one player in particular: Bill Russell. The issue was that the Celtics had the ninth pick in the draft, and Russell was projected to go first. Auerbach would not be deterred, so he got to work. The team with the first pick was the Rochester Royals. Auerbach promised them several "Ice Capades" shows at their arena with the condition that they would not take Russell at number one. Walter Brown was also a part owner of the Ice Capades and was able to make that promise.[13]

---

12 Larry Schwartz, "Celtics Tried to Pass on Ultimate Passer," *ESPN*, accessed May 10, 2020.

13 Hayden Bird, "How Red Auerbach Used the Ice Capades to Add Bill Russell to the Celtics' Best Draft Class," *Boston Globe*, June 22, 2016.

"Walter Brown was a prime stockholder in the Ice Capades, which was a big draw for all of these arenas. And he made a deal with Lester Harrison that if they (Rochester) did not take Russell, he would maneuver the Ice Capades and they would set up some dates for the Ice Capades to appear at Lester's arena. So, he's the only player in NBA history that got traded for the Ice Capades."

—TOMMY HEINSOHN[14]

At number two was the St. Louis Hawks. While Auerbach was progressive in his roster makeup, the rest of the league wasn't feeling it—especially in Jim Crow era St. Louis. Knowing this, Auerbach offered them a white, big man named Ed Macauley (a perennial All-Star, future Hall of Famer) and pick rights to someone else in return for the second pick. The Hawks agreed. Auerbach got his man and the Celtics dynasty officially started. Russell would go on to become a five-time NBA MVP and an eleven-time NBA Champion (the most in league history). He's a Hall of Famer and is still second in total rebounds all time.[15] He is not only one of the greatest Celtics, but one of the greatest NBA players of all time.

Russell was not the only player that the Celtics came away with in that 1956 draft. In fact, he wasn't even the first player they took. The Celtics used a now-defunct rule—the territorial pick—to claim Tommy Heinsohn before anyone was drafted.[16] Essentially, the way the territorial pick worked,

---

14 Ibid.
15 Ibid.
16 Chris Forsberg, "How Tommy Heinsohn Was Nearly Mr. Caterpillar Instead of Mr. Celtics," *NBC Sports*, April 29, 2020.

was that NBA teams could claim one "hometown" college player before they were drafted (this rule is so much fun and I wish it was still in the league in some capacity). Heinsohn played for Holy Cross and the Celtics claimed him before anyone else got a chance. Heinsohn was known primarily as a scorer, and he made six All-Star games in his career. He was inducted into the Hall of Fame and is credited with helping form the National Basketball Players Association (NBPA). He also won Rookie of the Year in 1957 over his teammate Bill Russell.

Before we keep trucking along, I should touch on two more players. Auerbach drafted Sam Jones before the 1957 season. Jones was known for his quickness and clutch shots, earning the nickname "Mr. Clutch." K.C. Jones was drafted before the 1958 season. He was known as a tenacious defender and would go on to coach the Larry Bird-era Celtics.[17] Both were inducted into the Hall of Fame after their respective retirements.

REVOLUTIONIZING THE GAME

Red Auerbach finally had the roster he wanted. Now, he had to get them to play the way he wanted. Many staples of Auerbach's play styles revolutionized the game at that time. They focused mainly on the transition game and what they called "the fast break," where Celtics players would quickly change directions from defense to offense after a stop. Led by Bob

---

17   "K.C. Jones Coaches Index," Basketball Reference, Sports Reference LLC, accessed May 10, 2020.

Cousy's incredible speed, Bill Russell's pinpoint outlet passes, and the overall team's ability to finish at the rim, the Celtics pulverized their opponents in transition.

Auerbach also popularized two of basketball's most unglamorous tasks: the role player and the sixth man. In terms of the role player Auerbach told reporters:

"That's a player who willingly undertakes the thankless job that has to be done in order to make the whole package fly."[18]

Basically "role players" are non-star players that have the responsibility to either give those stars support when they're on the court together or keep everything under control while those stars are resting on the bench. The "Other Guys" in basketball, as it were. Auerbach would often draft and acquire players with the intention of turning them into role players, a title that those players would graciously accept. The sixth man was another strategy of Auerbach's. When the other team's starters would begin to get tired, the Celtics would put in their sixth man—a player who compliments the other four starters perfectly and would dominate with fresh legs. Frank Ramsey, yet another Hall of Famer drafted by Auerbach, was the first player to be used like this and is often referred to as "the NBA's first sixth man." Ramsey would often come in at the end of close games, turning the tides on the Celtics' opponents.[19]

---

18   Lisette Hilton, "Auerbach's Celtics Played as a Team," *ESPN*, accessed May 10, 2020.

19   Ibid.

In 1962, Auerbach drafted future Hall of Famer, John Havlicek, to take over this role. Note, I'm only touching on Havlicek a bit here because he did most of his damage *after* this dynasty. However, to avoid being crucified by Boston, here are some quick hitters on him:

- Double digits in All-Star appearances and All-NBA teams selected
- All-time points leader in Celtics history
- Cream of NBA crop that many Celtics from this era are a part of

Lastly, Auerbach invented the concept of "the victory cigar." In today's game, the victory cigar usually refers to a bench player who gets no playing time being put in at the end of a blowout. Brian Scalabrine is probably the most well-known victory cigar player in NBA history, while famous bust Darko Milicic was actually called "The Human Victory Cigar" during his playing days.[20] Auerbach's victory cigar was much more literal. Toward the end of games where it became clear that the Celtics would win, Auerbach would light up a cigar right there on the bench.[21] It was the ultimate "fuck you" to the other team. Auerbach and his team were changing the way the game of basketball was played, they would change the way the league was run and viewed as well.

---

20 Jesse Dorsey, "The Top Human Victory Cigars in the NBA," *Bleacher Report*, January 10, 2012.

21 Tom Reed, "Defiance, Bragging: A History of Victory Cigars, from Red to MJ, Team Canada's Party, Buckeyes and Bama, LeBron and Steph," *The Athletic*, March 20, 2019.

RACE RELATIONS AND THE BOSTON CELTICS

The NBA wasn't necessarily a welcoming sport to African Americans in the 1950s and 1960s. It certainly wasn't anything like the progressive sports league it is today (arguably the most progressive in the US right now). Auerbach made history when he selected Chuck Cooper as the first drafted African American player, and it did not necessarily delight other teams. But that was Auerbach; he simply didn't care. Whoever was better was who he would play or choose.

Maybe that mentality came from some discrimination he faced as well. When Auerbach initially passed on Bob Cousy in 1950, he received several death threats. A number of them attacked his Jewish heritage. Among dozens of accolades, Auerbach is honored in the Jewish Sports Hall of Fame; his name has been enshrined for eternity. Auerbach was the first to draft an African American player and to field a starting lineup consisting solely of black players. He appointed Bill Russell as the first black head coach in American sports history when he retired in 1966.[22]

Russell himself was a civil rights leader at the time.

---

22 Lisette Hilton, "Auerbach's Celtics Played as a Team," *ESPN*, accessed May 10, 2020.

"Bill Russell, the man, is someone who stood up for the rights and dignity of all men. He marched with King; he stood by Ali. When a restaurant refused to serve the black Celtics, he refused to play in the scheduled game. He endured insults and vandalism, but he kept on focusing on making the teammates who he loved better players, and made possible the success of so many who would follow. And I hope that one day, in the streets of Boston, children will look up at a statue built not only to Bill Russell the player, but Bill Russell the man."

—BARACK OBAMA AWARDING BILL RUSSELL THE PRESIDENTIAL MEDAL OF FREEDOM IN 2011[23]

Now, this is not to say that Boston was an exception to the rest of the nation at the time. Russell and other players were harassed and had their homes broken into on several occasions. Russell famously asked to have his jersey retirement without Boston fans, just a small ceremony with friends and family.[24]

Despite being the greatest team in the league by far, the Celtics would rarely sell out games. When the team sent out a survey asking what would drive up attendance, an overwhelming amount of responses mentioned reducing the number of black players on the team.[25] Nonetheless, Red Auerbach and Bill Russell operated the way they wanted.

---

23 Kyle Boon, "Look: NBA Legend Bill Russell Takes a Knee with Presidential Medal of Freedom," *CBS Sports*, September 26, 2017.

24 Adam Himmelsbach, "Why Was Boston Garden Nearly Empty When Bill Russell's Number Was Retired in 1972?" *Boston Globe*, October 17, 2017.

25 Bill Simmons, "Mr. Russell's House," Filmed February 2013 in Seattle, WA. NBA TV Originals, 13:05.

DOMINANCE

The Red Auerbach-Bill Russell era Boston Celtics won eleven titles in thirteen seasons, including eight straight from 1959–66. They started their eight-year run by sweeping the Minneapolis Lakers in the Finals, a sort of "passing of the torch" from the first dynasty to the next. Here's a rundown of their titles:

- **1957:** Celtics sweep Syracuse Nationals 3–0 to advance to the Finals (they earned a bye). Celtics beat St. Louis Hawks 4–3 to win their first title. Bill Russell collected the most rebounds in the Finals and Bob Cousy had the most assists.
- **1958:** Celtics lose 2–4 to the Hawks in the Finals. Bill Russell missed two of the six Finals games due to injury. He still led the playoffs in rebounds. Cousy again led in assists.
- **1959:** Celtics beat Nationals 4–3 in the Eastern Division Finals. Celtics sweep the Minneapolis Lakers 4–0 in the Finals. Russell and Cousy repeat their achievements from the previous playoffs.
- **1960:** Celtics beat Philadelphia Warriors 4–2 in the Eastern Division Finals. Celtics beat Hawks 4–2 to capture their second straight title. Bill and Cousy again lead the playoffs in rebounds and points.
- **1961:** Celtics beat Nationals 4–1 to advance to the Finals. Celtics beat Hawks 4–1 in the Finals. Russell and Cousy do exactly what you think they did.
- **1962:** Celtics beat Warriors 4–3 in the Eastern Finals. Celtics beat the Los Angeles Lakers (they have now moved)

4–3 in the Finals. Do Russell and Cousy do the exact same thing? Yes, they do.

- **1963:** Celtics beat Royals 4–3 en route to the Finals. Celtics beat LA Lakers 4–2 to win the title. Russell and Cousy: Yep.
- **1964:** Celtics beat the newly moved-Cincinnati Royals 4–1 in the Eastern Division Finals. The Celtics beat the also newly moved-San Francisco Warriors 4–1 in the Finals (Boston beat teams into new cities and beat them there, how's that for disheartening). No Celtics lead the playoffs in points, rebounds, or assists.
- **1965:** Celtics beat the Philadelphia 76ers 4–3 to go to the Finals. Celtics beat the Lakers 4–1 to win yet again. Bill Russell leads the playoffs in both rebounds and assists.
- **1966:** Celtics beat the Royals 3–2 in the first round (first time they did not have a bye). Celtics beat 76ers 4–1 in the second round. Celtics take it to the Lakers yet again, 4–3, to win their eighth straight title.
- **1967:** Celtics lose 1–4 to the 76ers (led by Wilt Chamberlain) in the Eastern Division Finals. 76ers win the title.
- **1968:** Celtics beat Detroit Pistons 4–2 in the Eastern Division Semifinals. Celtics beat 76ers 4–3 in the Eastern Division Finals. Celtics beat Lakers 4–3 for another title. Bill Russell leads playoffs in rebounds. John Havlicek leads the playoffs in both points and assists.
- **1969:** Celtics beat 76ers 4–1 in the first round. Celtics beat Knicks 4–2 en route to the Finals. Celtics beat Lakers 4–3 for their eleventh and final title in this era. Jerry West is awarded the first Finals MVP award and remains the only player in NBA history to win the Finals MVP despite his

team losing.[26] No Celtics players led the playoffs in points, rebounds, or assists.

From 1957 to 1968, they would never finish below second in the Eastern Conference. They won at least 60 percent of their games every season of this run. They won Coach of the Year (Auerbach) and Rookie of the Year (Heinsohn) once in those thirteen seasons. They had six MVP awards (Cousy once and Russell five times) throughout the entirety of the run. Russell was also highly respected by his peers, as Celtics player Don Nelson told the *Boston Herald:*

"There are two types of superstars. One makes himself look good at the expense of the other guys on the floor. But there is another type who makes the players around him look better than they are, and that's the type Russell was."[27]

No team has been to more than five straight Finals (most recently done by the GSW dynasty) besides these Celtics, and they went to ten straight. Only four other teams have won three straight championships; none have even come close to the eight-straight record.

THE END OF AN ERA

Red Auerbach retired as head coach after the 1965–66 season and handed the reigns to Bill Russell, who would serve as

---

26 Ben Rohrbach, "Whose NBA Career Is Better? Stephen Curry vs. Jerry West," *Yahoo! Sports,* June 4, 2020.

27 "Bill Russell Biography," NBA Encyclopedia, Turner Sports Network, accessed May 10, 2020.

a player-coach. Auerbach remained the general manager of the Celtics until well into the 1980s.[28] Russell retired after they won the 1969 title, effectively ending the greatest run of dominance the NBA has ever seen. While the Celtics would compete (and even win more championships) in the '70s and '80s, this was the end of this historic iteration of the Celtics.

FINAL THOUGHTS

Again, we cannot really apply the formula to give this team a "dynasty score." Many of the accolades that I use in the formula are available for this team, but not some of the statistics. The use of now-defunct rules to build their team in the first place muddies things up as well. No worries; we can still use this team as a lesson.

Red Auerbach and the Celtics revolutionized the way basketball is played several times. If you think that cannot be done in the modern NBA, the Golden State Warriors and their small ball "death lineup" would like a word. Roster construction goes beyond ways to secure players; it involves who you are looking for. Auerbach and his players were as open-minded as they came in the 1960s. With no regard for color or any obstacle, the Celtics regularly pursued the best players, no matter who they were. This has been seen in modern times with NBA teams shying away from drafting European players; scouts and coaches have preferred American college players. Sometimes teams are right to shy away

---

28   Lisette Hilton, "Auerbach's Celtics Played as a Team," *ESPN*, accessed May 10, 2020.

from European players, but oftentimes preconceived notions get in the way.

Franchises that take the best player regardless of their background (Giannis Antetokounmpo to the Bucks and Luka Doncic to the Mavericks are some of the most recent examples) have found success in the modern NBA. Auerbach's regular preaching of team basketball and popularizing role players and sixth men also contributed to the sustained success of the franchise. It was easy to manage the personalities of numerous future Hall of Famers on the roster because they all focused on the same goal: winning. Players relished being the Celtics' role players and sixth men, so much so that they would come to Boston strictly for those roles. Being able to plug roster holes with players who were ready and willing to do the dirty work helped build around Russell and company for many years.

While the Celtics built a roster that seemingly churned out Hall of Famers by the second, it is in the culture and mentality of the team where we find the best help for building dynasties today. We will be traveling to the West Coast for the first time in our next chapter; it's Showtime baby!

FOREWORD TO PART 2:

MODERN ERA

All right guys, here's where we really start picking up steam. I'm sure you all have been foaming at the mouth to hear about this formula that I've been basically throwing in your face for the past couple of chapters. Well, I'm going to explain it now in the Foreword to Part 2 of *DYNASTY*.

Basically, there are eight categories. You can earn points in each category based on your team's and players' performances. A "bonus points" category exists, which I'll explain further down. After we have tallied up each category, we add it all up and divide by eight to assign that team a "dynasty score." Let's do some bullet points to break down each category.

CATEGORY 1: AWARDING TEAMS THAT ACQUIRE PEOPLE WHO KNOW HOW TO WIN.

- Add ten points for every player, coach, or general manager with "Dynasty DNA" on your roster.
- Someone with "Dynasty DNA" refers to anyone that won three or more titles with a different franchise before joining this current team.
- A perfect example of the bullet point above is Steve Kerr. He won three titles with the Chicago Bulls. Later on, he won two titles with the San Antonio Spurs. He would qualify as a "Dynasty DNA" player during those seasons on the Spurs. Even later on, he coached the Golden State Warriors and won three titles as the coach. He would qualify as a "Dynasty DNA" coach for those seasons.
- This only applies to players who contributed to the team (more details on this below), *head* coaches, and whoever is listed as the "Head Executive" for those seasons.

CATEGORY 2: SAME PURPOSE AS CATEGORY 1 ALONG WITH REWARDING RETENTION OF CHAMPIONSHIP WINNERS.

- Add five points for every "Proven Winner" on the roster.
- A "Proven Winner" is anyone who won two or fewer titles with a franchise before joining this current team.
- No one can qualify for both Category 1 and Category 2. If they won three or more, they belong in Category 1. If not, they belong in Category 2.
- This only applies to players who contributed to the team (more details on this below), *head* coaches, and whoever is listed as the "Head Executive" for those seasons.

- BONUS POINTS: Add one point for every player that was retained from the team's previous champions. If a team won in '91, every player that was on that '91 team that remained on the '92 team would be worth one extra point.

CATEGORY 3: AWARDING TEAMS FOR DRAFTING THEIR OWN PLAYERS.

- Add five points for every player on the roster that was drafted by the team.
- This only qualifies for players that were drafted and stayed on the team. If they left at one point and are now back on the team, they do not qualify.
- Coaches and executives do not qualify.

CATEGORY 4: AWARDING TEAMS FOR ACQUIRING ALL-STARS.

- Add fifteen points for every All-Star on the roster for the *current* season—not reigning All-Stars, only current season All-Stars.

CATEGORY 5: AWARDING TEAMS FOR ACQUIRING TOP FIFTEEN PLAYERS.

- Add twenty points for any All-NBA player on the roster. First, Second, and Third Teams all qualify.
- A player cannot qualify for both Category 4 and Category 5. If they made both, they only qualify for Category 5.

CATEGORY 6: AWARDING TEAMS FOR ACQUIRING TOP TEN DEFENSIVE PLAYERS.

- Add fifteen points for every All-Defensive player on the roster. First and Second Teams both qualify.
- Players can double up on points here! Because an All-Defensive selection doesn't guarantee either an All-Star or All-NBA selection, a player that makes both gets points for both. If a player makes all three, they only qualify for points in Category 5 and Category 6.

CATEGORY 7: AWARDING TEAMS FOR ACQUIRING HIGH-LEVEL ROLE PLAYERS TO PAIR WITH THEIR STARS.

- Add ten points for every non-All-Star, All-NBA, or All-Defensive player on the roster with a BPM (Box Plus-Minus)* of +2 or higher.
- Every catch-all stat has its fatal flaws, but I like the way BPM measures role/reserve player performances, so that's what I chose.

CATEGORY 8: AWARDING TEAMS FOR ACQUIRING SOLID ROLE PLAYERS TO BACK UP THEIR STARS.

- Add five points for every non-All-Star, non-All-NBA, or non-All-Defensive player on the roster with a BPM of at least -2 all the way up to +2.

BONUS POINTS:

- Add twenty-five points if you have the regular season MVP on your roster.
- Add twenty points if you have the Defensive Player of the Year, Sixth Man of the Year, or Most Improved Player on your roster.
- Add fifteen points if you have the Coach of the Year or Rookie of the Year on your roster.

After you add up all the categories, that number divided by eight is that season's "Dynasty Score" for that team. The way we're going to compare dynasties is to compare their average "Dynasty Scores." We're trying to take the average dynasty score (DS) of the team when it was contending, not necessarily during the building of the team. In that spirit, the average will take the DS of every season starting with the specific team's first championship all the way to the last Finals appearance for that iteration of the team.

A couple of extra rules:

- A "role player" is defined as any non-All-Star, All-NBA, or All-Defense player on the roster that contributes to the team.
- "Contributing" means either averaging at least twelve minutes (a quarter of a game) per game for more than half of the regular season, *or* if you were picked up later in the season (due to late season trade or late season buyout free agents), you have to average at least twelve minutes a game after your acquisition *and* at least ten minutes a game in the playoffs.

- If you win 6MOY, ROY, or MIP but don't make any of the All-Star, All-NBA, or All-Defense teams, you can still qualify for Category 7 or Category 8.
- You have to have played this season to qualify for anything. Kevin Durant has not played a minute for the Nets, so he wouldn't qualify for the "Proven Winner" section despite his time on Golden State.

Here is an explanation of BPM from Basketball-Reference

Box Plus/Minus, Version 2.0 (BPM) is a basketball box score-based metric that estimates a basketball player's contribution to the team when that player is on the court. It is based only on the information in the traditional basketball box score; no play-by-play data or nontraditional box score data (like dunks or deflections) are included.

League average is defined as 0.0, meaning zero points above average or below average. Because above-average players play more minutes, there are far more below-average players than above-average players in the league at any time. A value of +5.0 means the team is five points per one hundred possessions better with the player on the floor than with average production from another player. (In the 2018–19 season, teams averaged around one hundred possessions per forty-eight-minute game.)

To give a sense of the scale:

+10.0 is an all-time season (think peak Jordan or LeBron)

+8.0 is an MVP season (think peak Dirk or Shaq)

+6.0 is an all-NBA season

+4.0 is in All-Star consideration

+2.0 is a good starter

+0.0 is a decent starter or solid sixth man

-2.0 is a bench player (this is also defined as "replacement level")

Below -2.0 are many end-of-bench players[29]

From now on, each chapter will end with this formula being run for the specific team and a discussion of the results. Season by season, average, and interesting tidbits will all be examined. Let's apply it to our first dynasty with more than twelve teams in the league (the league had twelve teams in Bill Russell's last season, but actually had fewer than ten for much of that dynasty's run).

---

29 Daniel Myers, "About Box Plus/Minus (BPM)," *Basketball Reference*, February 2020.

CHAPTER 3:

THE SHOWTIME LAKERS

———

After the Bill Russell Celtics, a bit of a dynasty drought occurred. Dynasties usually pop up at least once or twice a decade, but it would take about a full decade before the next one revealed itself. In between that, teams traded championships like they were Luke Ridnour. (If you don't already know, Luke Ridnour was traded four times in the span of a week in the summer of 2015; there are rules in place to ensure it doesn't happen again.)[30] The Milwaukee Bucks, Seattle Supersonics (now the Oklahoma City Thunder), Washington Bullets (now the Wizards), and Portland Trail Blazers all got their first and only titles during this dynasty drought. The New York Knicks won two championships in this state of flux, which is a surprising thing to read if you've followed the Knicks since... well those championships, I guess (it's been hard times for Dolan and the Knicks). In 1975–76, the Lakers began building their second dynasty, the first in Los Angeles.

---

30   Chuck Schilken, "NBA Journeyman Luke Ridnour Is Traded to His Fifth Team in Six Days," *Los Angeles Times*, June 30, 2015.

Why were they called the Showtime Lakers? The name has dual roots in the play style of the team and the ownership of Jerry Buss. Buss wanted his team to reflect the Los Angeles and Hollywood lifestyle, and he delivered on that. He insisted that the team play an up-tempo style of ball, which showcased Magic Johnson and Kareem Abdul-Jabbar's talents perfectly. He hired a live band and dancers (they were the first team to have cheerleaders in the NBA) to make it a more "Hollywood" experience.[31] He enticed the many celebrities in Los Angeles to come to the games, many of them becoming fans for decades (for example, Jack Nicholson). That's how the Lakers became known as Showtime, and this is how they were built.

THE BIG MAN PRINCIPLE

The summer before the 1975 season began included a sad moment for the Laker franchise. Longtime Laker great, Jerry West (get used to this name), retired. The next move they made, however, would change the trajectory of the franchise forever. They traded Dave Meyers (the second overall pick in that year's draft), Junior Bridgeman (the eighth overall pick in that year's draft), and Brian Winters (an all-star the season after he was traded) to the Milwaukee Bucks in return for superstar center Kareem Abdul-Jabbar.

Kareem was a three-time league MVP when he was traded and was awarded the Finals MVP when he won the

---

31   James Pasley, "How Cheerleading Evolved from One Man Yelling in Minnesota to 4.5 Million Leaping Cheerleaders," *Business Insider*, January 31, 2020.

championship with the Bucks in 1971. While he was a massive individual talent, he always had a respect and emphasis for team basketball:

"We have all witnessed sports teams in which one run-and-gun player consistently scores a tremendous amount of points, but the team still mostly loses. That player, clearly chasing a sports shoe endorsement, has never learned to put the benefit of the team above personal gratification. They don't understand that—here comes another sports platitude—'The rising tide lifts all boats.' When the team wins, each member of that team benefits more. Being a star player on a losing team focuses the blame on you."

—KAREEM[32]

Exposition Time!

Milwaukee wasn't known as a super-welcoming community for African Americans in the '70s (or even now to an extent).[33] Kareem spoke out once or twice about the issues in Milwaukee and faced serious backlash for it. Kareem was born in New York City and went to college in Los Angeles; he always desired to be in a big city. Those two factors culminated in KAJ respectfully asking for a trade.[34]

---

32 Kareem Abdul-Jabbar, "What My Life in Sports Has Taught Me," *Thought Economics*, July 17, 2019.

33 John Schmid, "Milwaukee's Trauma Care Initiatives Are Meant to Heal. Now They Are at the Heart of the City's Racial Divide," *Milwaukee Journal Sentinel*, June 18, 2019.

34 Thomas Bonk, "June 16, 1975: A Banner Day for Lakers," *Los Angeles Times*, December 25, 1987.

The Bucks sent him to Los Angeles. The Lakers did not make the playoffs that season and Kareem ended up being the only player on the current roster that would still be on the team when they won the championship later on (I get that them winning is kind of a spoiler but you should have figured that out when I wrote a chapter about these guys). Despite missing the playoffs, Kareem secured his fourth MVP award along with being named to the All-NBA First Team and the All-Defense Second Team.

GROWING PAINS

In 1976–77, the Lakers brought Jerry West back into the organization as the head coach. He immediately became frustrated in his new role when the Lakers wouldn't sign off on the amount of money it would have taken to sign Julius "Dr. J" Irving, who was being openly sold at the time. The Nets had to pay to go from the ABA to the NBA, and the amount was so high they had to sell their best player to cover the costs.[35] In addition to that, the Lakers lost five-time All-Star Gail Goodrich to the New Orleans Jazz (old teams are fun, and their names actually make sense). However, the NBA rules at the time stipulated that the Lakers be compensated for their lost asset, similar to how the NFL works today. For losing a player of Goodrich's caliber, the Lakers got three of the Jazz's future first-round picks (stay tuned).[36] The Lakers went 53–29 and earned a bye as the first seed (how the playoffs

---

35   Steve Aschburner, "Larry Bird, Magic Johnson Lifted the NBA with Heated Rivalry," *NBA*, December 28, 2019.

36   Steve Politi, "Who Knows What Nets Could Have Been If Dr. J Stayed?" *NJ.com*, March 30, 2019.

worked back then). They beat the Golden State Warriors in a grueling seven games before being swept by Portland. Kareem repeated all the accolades he had the season prior, including league MVP.

The 1977–78 season was a disaster and a disgrace for the Lakers. In the off-season they drafted Norm Nixon at twenty-second overall and signed Jamaal Wilkins, two players who would play meaningful minutes for the Lakers in the coming years. The good decisions ended there. Two minutes into the first game of the season, Kareem punched Milwaukee Bucks player Kent Benson in the face and broke his hand.[37] KAJ would be out of action for two months. On December 9, in the middle of another skirmish, Lakers player Kermit Washington punched four-time All-Star Rudy Tomjanovich (now a Hall of Fame inductee). Tomjanovich was charging at Washington at full speed, so when the punch stopped him dead in his tracks, the results were devastating. So devastating, in fact, that Tomjanovich was nearly medically retired due to his injuries.[38] Washington was suspended for sixty games and the Lakers traded him two weeks later to the Boston Celtics. The Lakers went 45–37 and lost their first-round matchup to Seattle. They had no All-Stars that season.

The Lakers continued to add to their young core the following season (1978–79). They drafted Michael Cooper in

---

37 Paul L. Montgomery, "Abdul-Jabbar Fined $5,000 for One Punch," *The New York Times*, October 21, 1977.

38 Chris Cobbs, "The Punch: Tomjanovich and Washington Both Still Feel the Pain from That Terrible Moment," *Los Angeles Times*, January 28, 1985.

the third round (yeah, third round was around back then). They went 47–35 and beat Denver 2–1 in their opening series before falling again to the Seattle Supersonics in five games. Kareem was an All-Star and was named to the All-NBA Second Team, as well as the All-Defense First Team.

Note:
From this point on, if a player made any All-NBA team, I probably will not be mentioning that they also made the All-Star team. Every All-NBA player pretty much makes the All-Star game, but not always the other way around. This does not extend to All-Defensive players; they sometimes make the All-Star roster and sometimes don't.

RIGHT PLACE RIGHT TIME

Remember when the Lakers got three first-round draft picks from the Jazz as compensation for losing Gail Goodrich? Well, they whiffed on the first two. But in the 1979 draft, the pick they had from the Jazz ended up being the number one overall pick. They took Magic Johnson. The Lakers got Magic fucking Johnson from a compensation pick! Oh, to be a basketball franchise with good luck. This off-season was brimming with change and Magic was just the beginning. Dr. Jerry Buss bought the Lakers and immediately began an intense friendship with Magic.

"One of my first friends in Los Angeles was the new owner, Jerry Buss," wrote Magic in his autobiography.[39]

Buss reassigned Jerry West to a scout position in the organization and hired Jack McKinney as the head coach. He would only last fifteen games, however, as a bicycle injury would force Paul Westhead in as interim head coach for the remainder of the season.[40] The Lakers made six trades before and during the 1979–80 season. For everyone's sanity (especially mine), let's do some bullet points for the four trades that had an actual impact on the team:

- **Trade #1:** Adrian Dantley to the Utah Jazz (yep, first year in Utah) in return for star power forward Spencer Haywood (Stay tuned for part two).
- **Trade #2:** Dave Robisch and a third-round draft pick to the Cleveland Cavaliers in return for backup center Jim Chones.
- **Trade #3:** Ollie Mack and two second-round draft picks to the Chicago Bulls for backup big man Mark Landsberger.
- **Trade #4:** Don Ford and a first-round draft pick to the Cleveland Cavaliers in return for Butch Lee (averaged one point per game which, congrats) and a future first-round draft pick (Stay Tuned: Trilogy, strap in!).

Magic Johnson was an instant stud. In his rookie season, he was named to the All-Rookie First Team and the All-Star team. Kareem won his sixth MVP award, an all-time record. The Lakers went 60–22 and again earned a bye as the first

39   Earvin "Magic" Johnson, *My Life* (New York: Fawcett Books, 1992), 105.
40   Helene Elliott, "Jack McKinney's Bike Ride Changed Lakers' History," *Los Angeles Times*, February 9, 2012.

seed. They only dropped one game apiece in their first two series against the Phoenix Suns and the Supersonics en route to the Finals. There, they would meet the Philadelphia 76ers, who were led by Dr. J (they were the team that eventually paid up for the Nets' stud). During the Finals, Spencer Haywood was dismissed by the team for falling asleep during a practice due to his intense cocaine addiction (that was a worthwhile "stay tuned" wasn't it?).[41]

Despite the distractions, Kareem dominated the series. He led both teams in rebounds in all five games and in points for four of the five. Nothing could stop him. Well, not the other team at least. Late in game five, Kareem went down with a severely sprained ankle. He would not be able to play in game six. With a 3–1 lead and facing a desperate 76ers team that suddenly saw hope, it came down to rookie Magic Johnson. He, normally the starting point guard, started at center for the injured Kareem. He seemed ready as well:

"[He] sat in Abdul-Jabbar's seat, winked at coach Paul West-head and announced to the team, 'Never fear, E.J. is here.'"[42]

All he did was put up forty-two points and fifteen rebounds in a near blowout to secure the championship. For his efforts, he was named the Finals MVP, the youngest player ever and the only rookie ever to be given the award. The Lakers had two of the top ten players in the league and they were only getting started.

---

41 Rob Trucks, "Why I Thought About Killing My NBA Head Coach (and Why I Didn't Do it)," *Deadspin*, March 14, 2014.

42 Rhiannon Walker, "The Day Magic Johnson Stepped in at Center and Dropped 42 Points on Philly," *The Undefeated*, May 16, 2018.

MORE BUILDING

The Lakers were champions, but they were not yet a dynasty. They were a couple moves away, along with development from their young guys, from reaching that level of success. It did not help that Magic would miss more than half the 1980–81 season with a knee injury. Despite the loss of Magic, the Lakers went 54–28. They were led by a rejuvenated Kareem Abdul-Jabbar.

He was named First Team for both All-NBA and All-Defense. The Lakers were also helped by two young guys coming into their own. Jamaal Wilkins was an All-Star and Michael Cooper was named to the All-Defense Second Team, both new additions to their resumes. The Lakers fell in the first round of the playoffs to the Houston Rockets, led by the dominant Moses Malone (top five coolest NBA names of all time, no arguments allowed).

Mitch Kupchak was signed as the team's starting power forward before the 1981–82 season. He played well but went down with an ugly knee injury after twenty-six games. He would miss nearly two seasons of action rehabbing. The team signed Kurt Rambis as his replacement.

Fun Fact!

Both Kupchak and Rambis have held important front office positions for the Lakers following their playing careers.

They also traded a second-rounder for Bob McAdoo. The future Hall of Famer was in his twilight years by now, but he served well as a backup center.

The 1981–82 season was not without its drama, however.

Early in the season, Magic Johnson requested a trade due to Paul Westhead's boring, restrictive offense. He made his demand public to reporters after an early game in Utah:

"I can't play here anymore. I want to leave. I want to be traded."[43]

Jerry Buss, who would have rather died than see Magic on another team, promptly fired Westhead. He named Jerry West and Pat Riley (a former Laker player who had served as Westhead's lead assistant coach) as "co-coaches." His intention was for West to be the "main" co-coach and for Riley to be his "side" (but *not* assistant) co-coach. Confusing, I know. Jerry West agreed and took matters into his own hands, telling reporters during a press conference:

"I'm going to work for Pat, this will not be a permanent situation for me. I will feel much more confident with Pat taking over. He has ideas and I have ideas."[44]

He named Riley as the actual head coach without Buss's knowledge. It worked out for them, though, as Pat Riley's

43 AP, "Lakers Drop Westhead as Coach," *The New York Times*, November 20, 1981

44 Rhiannon Walker, "The Day Magic Johnson Stepped in at Center and Dropped 42 Points on Philly," *The Undefeated*, May 16, 2018.

new offense freed up space for Magic Johnson to, well, work his magic. The team went 57–25, swept Phoenix and San Antonio in the first two rounds, and once again beat the 76ers in six games to secure the championship. Magic was again named the Finals MVP while he, Norm Nixon, and Kareem were all All-Stars. Michael Cooper made his debut on the All-Defense First Team.

RIGHT PLACE RIGHT TIME (AGAIN)

Hey, remember when the Lakers traded Don Ford and a first-rounder to the Cavaliers for a bench guy and a future first? Well, that future first was for the 1982 draft, which was the first overall pick. Again. So, the Lakers took James Worthy, yet another future Hall of Famer. This time it was Jerry West making the draft pick, as he was promoted to general manager in the offseason. Worthy would make the All-Rookie First Team despite breaking his leg in the first week of the season. The Lakers went 55–27 and earned a bye. They lost just one game to the Trail Blazers and beat the Spurs in six games. They set up a rematch with the 76ers in the Finals, the third time in four seasons and the second straight time they had met in the Finals. These were not the same old 76ers; however, they had traded for Moses Malone (a known Lakers kryptonite) before the season. Would the addition make a difference? Yes, it did, and the Lakers were swept. Moses Malone was named the Finals MVP.

Jerry West decided it was time for some changes before the 1983–84 season. He traded Eddie Jordan, Norm Nixon, and two second-rounders for the fourth overall pick in the

1983 draft: combo guard Byron Scott. The team went 54–28. Kareem Abdul Jabbar, at age thirty-six, was named to the All-NBA First Team and the All-Defense Second Team. Magic joined him on the First Team All-NBA roster. Byron Scott was named to the All-Rookie First Team (their *fifth* All-Rookie player in just seven seasons). Cooper maintained his First Team All-Defense slot.

The Lakers swept the Kansas City Kings (now the Sacramento Kings) in the first round and lost just one game to the Dallas Mavericks in the second round. They met the Phoenix Suns in the Conference Finals and beat them in six games. They met their ultimate foe, the Boston Celtics, in the Finals. At the time, the Lakers were 0–7 against the Celtics in the Finals. To call it a rivalry was giving the Lakers too much credit. The Lakers gave a valiant fight, but eventually caved due to Boston's physicality and Larry Bird's all-time clutch shots. They lost in seven games; the seventh game being played in Boston. The curse continued for the Lakers.

DYNASTY MENTALITY

The 1984–85 Lakers were on a mission. Embarrassed by their loss to the Celtics in the previous season, they had just one goal in mind: Beat Boston. They knew they were going to make the Finals and they knew they were likely going to meet Boston there. They just wanted to get there so they could grapple with them again. The team went 62–20 despite losing Jamaal Wilkins halfway through the season to injury. When they arrived at the playoffs, they simply made the other teams go away. The Lakers swept the Suns, lost one game to Portland, and lost one game to Denver.

They made it to the Finals, so did the Celtics. Here was the matchup they wanted, the one they needed. They lost Game one by thirty-four points. That game is known historically as the "Memorial Day Massacre" (not related to the *actual* Memorial Day Massacre, which was an *actual* tragedy).[45] Kareem was beaten up all game and he was declared "officially washed" by the media pundits after the game. At thirty-eight years old, it was possible that Father Time had finally caught up with him. Or, maybe not (this is what's known in the biz as a *misdirect*). Kareem took charge and led the Lakers to win four of the next five. They had finally beaten Boston, and in Boston no less. Kareem had twenty-nine points and seven rebounds in the series clincher. Magic Johnson gathered a triple double and youngster James Worthy scored twenty-eight points. Kareem won the Finals MVP, the oldest player in history to win the award. Buss famously said after the winning game:

"This has removed the most odious sentence in the English language. It can never again be said that the Lakers have never beaten the Celtics."[46]

The Lakers were not standing pat for the 1985–86 season. Wilkins walked in free agency and the team drafted A.C. Green at twenty-third overall to supplant the lost production.

---

45   Darren Hartwell, "This Date in Celtics History: C's Crush Lakers in 'Memorial Day Massacre,'" *NBC SPORTS*, May 27, 2020.

46   Seth Hojnacki, "Photo Timeline of Storied LA Lakers-Boston Celtics Rivalry," *Bleacher Report*, February 20, 2013.

They also traded two seconds (one of which was eventually used to take Steve Kerr, stay tuned: next chapter edition) to get some extra muscle off the bench in the form of Maurice Lucas. They went 62–20 again. Kareem became the oldest player in league history to be named to the First Team All-NBA. James Worthy was named to the All-Star game for the first time. Cooper and Magic had their usual great personal accolades. They swept the Spurs in the first round and beat the Mavericks in six games in the second round. They met their third straight Texas opponent (Houston Rockets) in the Conference Finals. They were popped in the mouth and lost in five games, thanks to a Ralph Sampson buzzer beater in Game 5.

In 1986–87, the Lakers moved A.C. Green into the starting lineup. He may not have made an All-Rookie team the year before, but he still continued the tradition of brilliant drafting by Jerry West and company. They also traded for Mychal Thompson (father of current NBA star Klay Thompson) and signed Wes Matthews (father of the current Milwaukee Buck by the same name). The team went 65–17 and Magic Johnson won his first league MVP award. Michael Cooper, among years of excellent defense, finally won the Defensive Player of the Year award. They lost just one total game in the first three rounds of the playoffs, beating the Nuggets, Warriors, and Supersonics.

In the Finals, they met the Celtics again, who had beaten the Rockets last season to win the title. They wanted the rematch last season, but the Lakers could not hold up their part of the deal. No matter, the rematch was on this season. The Lakers took the first two games, including a blowout in Game 2.

The teams traded wins until it came back down to Game 6 and the Lakers were able to pull it off yet again. Kareem scored thirty-two points, Worthy scored twenty-two points, and Magic garnered a sixteen-point, nineteen-assist double in the series clincher. The Lakers were finally giving some credibility to the league's greatest rivalry. Magic paired his MVP trophy with his second Finals MVP award.

Pat Riley, speaking to fans at the Lakers' victory parade announced: *"I'm guaranteeing to everybody here, we're going to win it again."* This was a bold prediction considering that no one had repeated as champions in over twenty years.[47]

The Lakers ran it back for the 1987–88 season, intent on backing Riley's promise. With no major changes to the roster, they went 62–20 and swept the Spurs in the first round. The wear and tear of years of deep playoff runs seemed to finally be getting to the team, however. They struggled in the second round against a Utah Jazz team that had twenty-five-year-old John Stockton and twenty-four-year-old Karl Malone on it. Experience won out in the end, as the Lakers took the series in seven games.

In the Conference Finals, they met the Dallas Mavericks. The Mavs were not as young as the Jazz team, but they had several stars that were smack dab in the middle of their primes. Roy Tarpley, their starting center, had nearly double the rebounds that the leading rebounder for the Lakers had in the series. The Lakers were again able to squeak out a Game 7 win.

---

47   Zack Pumerantz, "The 50 Best Trash Talk Lines in Sports History," *Bleacher Report*, June 29, 2012.

Finally, they met a brutal Pistons team in the Finals. They were a devastatingly physical team who prioritized defense first. Their leading scorer was Adrian Dantley, who the Lakers had traded for Spencer Haywood (oof) all those years ago. The Pistons won the two games in which Dantley was the leading scorer. It was Dantley versus Worthy for much of the series. Dantley put up thirty-four points to win Game 1, and Worthy scored twenty-six to win Game 2. It went on like that until it came down to yet another Game 7. The Lakers were running ragged; this was the longest playoffs they'd had in this iteration of the team. Worthy came up big, putting up a thirty-six-point triple-double (the only triple-double of his career!) in Game 7 and the Lakers were able to fulfill Pat Riley's prophecy. Worthy was awarded the Finals MVP for his efforts, marking the third player on that roster to earn that achievement. He also earned the nickname "Big Game James" for his heroics in that Game 7.

WHAT GOES UP...

The Lakers ran it back yet again in 1988–89. They were regular season beasts again, going 57–25. They swept every single team they met (Portland, Seattle, Phoenix) en route to the Finals. They met the Pistons again and were no match this time. Byron Scott missed the whole series with a hamstring injury and Magic, who was named the regular season MVP, missed game four with the same. The Lakers were swept. Kareem Abdul-Jabbar retired after the season at forty-one years old, marking the end of one of the absolute best careers in NBA history.

In 89–90, Magic repeated as the MVP and Pat Riley won Coach of the Year for the first time. The team went 63–19, a juggernaut again. They beat Houston in four games but lost to the Suns, who they had beaten up so many times over the years, in five games. Michael Cooper retired after the season. Pat Riley stepped down as coach. They would get another chance at a title in the near future, but this Lakers dynasty as we knew it was finished.

FINAL THOUGHTS

The Showtime Lakers exhibited some of the all-time best drafting during their run as a dynasty. They had a record of five straight seasons with six or more drafted contributing players among the dynasties we are examining. They are the only team to have seven drafted contributing players in a season (1986). While some would argue that they got lucky with two number-one overall picks, it was shrewd trading that got them those selections. They drafted five First Team All-Rookie players in a seven-year span, something that hasn't really been seen since. They drafted Michael Cooper, an all-time defensive player, in the third round of the draft.

Jerry West was always looking forward while also making short-term plays to ensure the strength of the roster was always high. Jerry Buss was always willing to spend to make sure they had a championship team. That kind of harmony in the front office cannot be understated. The Lakers also made the hard choice of firing their championship coach in favor of Pat Riley, whose coaching style fit the Lakers beautifully. It all started with the trade for Kareem Abdul-Jabbar, one of the

All-Time best players. Without him, none of this would have happened. The Lakers did the best job possible surrounding him with talent. Drafting, trades, and perfect personnel decisions. That is the legacy of the Showtime Lakers.

Looking at the formula, we are taking the Showtime Lakers average from their first title in 1980 all the way to their Finals appearance in 1989. They actually make it to the Finals in 1991, just two years after, but I decided not to include that in the formula average because the Lakers had two new starters, three new bench guys, and a new coach. I think the dynasty truly ended after the team lost Kareem and Riley. Their best season, according to the formula, was in 1987 (DS = 20.125), the year they went 65–17 and beat the Boston Celtics in six games. That also happened to be the year that Magic Johnson won his third regular season MVP award and Michael Cooper won his first (and only) Defensive Player of the Year award. Those two factors helped improve the dynasty score immensely, though they were aided with six drafted contributed players along with six returners from previous championships. Jerry West's success as a player qualified him as a "Proven Winner" for the entirety of the formula calculations. The Lakers' average dynasty score over the ten seasons of the dynasty was 16.6. This is a lower average score (lowest out of the five we examined, in fact) that can be attributed partially to the Lakers' injury troubles and to the fact that Showtime ran for ten seasons. (Name me a show that ran for ten seasons and all seasons are good. You can't.) It was Showtime's stars that gave that team its shine, but it cannot be understated how important the continuous flow of contributing draft picks to support them every year was.

EPILOGUE

In the 1990–91 season, the Lakers trotted out a team of experienced players mainly in their prime. Kareem-Abdul Jabbar and Michael Cooper may have been gone, but Magic, James Worthy, Byron Scott, and A.C. Green remained. Kareem's successor (for the season at least) was a young, European big man by the name of Vlade Divac (now the general manager for the Sacramento Kings). Divac was a skilled center with incredible touch and basketball IQ. He was an apt pick and roll partner for Magic Johnson. The new construction of the Lakers was still good, going 58–24 and second in their division. They swept the Rockets in the first round and dropped just one game against the Warriors in the second round. They met the up-and-coming Trail Blazers in the Conference Finals. The Lakers were able to squeak by in Game 6 by one point to win the series 3–2. It looked like the Lakers dynasty was going to add yet another ring in 1991. They won the first game but lost four straight afterward to the man that would rule the 90s: Michael fucking Jordan (a tad intense sure, but what an introduction).

CHAPTER 4:

HIS ROYAL AIRNESS AND THE CHICAGO BULLS DYNASTY

———

Some of these chapters have fun names and some of them don't; please keep up. If we're talking dynasties, we're talking the Chicago Bulls and Michael Jordan. The Celtics won eleven titles in thirteen years and the Warriors dynasty beat the Bulls all-time regular season record, but somehow the Bulls' accomplishments shine brighter. Maybe it's because they were the face of both the NBA and pop culture for nearly a decade. Maybe it's an internal bias that I haven't yet rectified. It's probably a mix of both.

Regardless, the Chicago Bulls (led by Michael Jordan) three-peated twice in an eight-year period. Jordan basically did not play in the two years between their titles. Either three-peat would have qualified them for dynasty status, but what they did gives them an argument for the best dynasty.

It's true that the Bulls drafted quite possibly the best player of all time (I'm not here to have arguments, please tweet at me with any concerns). It would be easy to discount their success as a dynasty considering they had that player, but the Bulls did something that is rarely done. They recognized the talent they had right away and built around those players from the start.

THE EARLY YEARS

The Bulls had the third pick in the 1984 draft. Hakeem Olajuwon was the consensus number one pick, and for good reason. He was a transcendent center at the time and is one of the best of all time. The Blazers, somewhat surprisingly, selected Sam Bowie over Michael Jordan (MJ) at number two. Bowie had been a known commodity since high school and was a very talented big man. The selection was made because the Blazers had drafted Clyde Drexler, a young star and a future Hall of Famer, the season prior. He happened to play the same position as Michael Jordan.

Even MJ agreed:

"He [Bowie] fits in better than I would. They have an overabundance of big guards and small forwards."[48]

Unfortunately, the pick did not work out. Bowie suffered a litany of injuries, never found footing in the NBA, and is

---

48 NBA.com Staff, "Legends Profile: Michael Jordan," *NBA History*, accessed June 4, 2020.

regarded as one of the biggest busts in NBA history. And so MJ fell to the Bulls.

Jordan was considered a sure thing coming out of college, and it was evident why almost immediately. Jordan was named the Rookie of the Year, made the All-NBA second team, and was a starter in the All-Star game his rookie year. Only three players since MJ have been starters in the All-Star game as rookies. He was also third in the NBA in points per game. They made the playoffs in his first year, but they lost in four games to the Milwaukee Bucks. After that season, massive changes came to the Bulls organization. Jerry Reinsdorf bought the Bulls, and Jerry Krause replaced the man who drafted Jordan as the general manager. They decided collectively that MJ was the future of the organization, and they were going to build around him.

Before the season, the Bulls traded a role player and their first-round pick to move up two spots and select Charles Oakley with the ninth pick in the 1985 draft. They signed John Paxson to become their new starting point guard. The 1985–86 season was a lost one for Jordan. He broke his left foot and missed sixty-four games, which was almost the entire season. Despite Jordan's injury, the Bulls still made the playoffs. Jordan was able to return for the playoffs and averaged a god-like 43.7 points per game, including a single game playoff record of sixty-three points in Game 2.

Jordan's legend was growing. In response to MJ's Game 2 explosion, Larry Bird famously remarked:

"God disguised as Michael Jordan."[49]

Despite the heroics, the Bulls were swept 3–0 by the Boston Celtics. The new front office decided there were more changes to be made.

THE COLLINS YEARS

Before the 1986–87 season, the Bulls fired Stan Albeck and hired Doug Collins, a first-time coach, as his successor. Collins was a disciplinarian who preached defense and hustle. Jordan was already a fiery competitor, but now he had a coach that matched his personality. The Bulls added ten more wins to their previous season's record, and Jordan led the league in scoring for the first time (37.09 points per game). This would be the first of *seven* straight scoring titles (an all-time record). Charles Oakley led the league in rebounds per game. MJ was the first Bull ever to be named to the All-NBA first team. Despite all this, the Bulls were again swept by the Boston Celtics in the first round. The Bulls were furious, but understood the team needed to improve. They would accomplish this with a treasure of first-round picks.

The 1987 draft changed the trajectory for the Chicago Bulls from bright future to scorching. They drafted Olden Polynice with the eighth pick and Horace Grant with the tenth pick. They then turned around and flipped Polynice, a future second-round pick, and a future first-round pick for the fifth pick in that draft (Scottie Pippen) and a future

---

49 Ibid.

first. Their starters remained relatively the same for that season, but they had a hoard of young guys on the bench ready to contribute.

While the draft changed the trajectory of the team, the 1987–88 season is when Michael Jordan introduced himself as the best player on the planet. It was his second straight year leading the league in scoring (34.98 points per game). He made first team All-NBA for the second straight year and was named first team All-Defense for the first time.

The personal accolades came as well. Jordan was the Most Valuable Player, the All-Star MVP, and the Defensive Player of the Year. Jordan was the first and now one of just two players in NBA history to win MVP and DPOY in the same year (Olajuwon did it twice). He is the only player in history to add All-Star MVP in the same year. Charles Oakley led the league in rebounds for the second straight season. Jerry Krause was rewarded for his efforts with the Executive of the Year award. The personal accolades were nice, but finally, the accomplishments led to playoff success. Michael Jordan won his first playoff series that year, beating the Cavaliers in a close one. MJ's "The Shot" over Craig Ehlo ended the series, further entrenching Jordan in basketball lore.[50] They were handled quite easily in the next round by the Detroit Pistons, however. Despite the loss, the Bulls were clearly improving.

The biggest need for the Bulls entering the 1988–89 season was a center. At the same time, the Bulls had an overabundance at power forward due to Horace Grant's rapid

---

50 Ibid.

development. The Bulls elected to trade Charles Oakley, a first-round pick, and a third-round pick to the New York Knicks in return for Bill Cartwright, a first, and a third. Cartwright's best days were behind him when he was traded to the Bulls, but he was perfectly serviceable as a starting center and would contribute in that spot for the first three of the Bulls' championships. Moving up in the first round, they selected Will Purdue, who added more depth to the center position. They also traded for Craig Hodges to be a three-point sniper off the bench.

Fun Fact!

Hodges participated in the first eight three-point contests in the NBA.

The new starting lineup of John Paxson, MJ, Scottie Pippen, Horace Grant, and Bill Cartwright would win forty-seven games and two playoff series. They had two close matchups with the Cavs and the Knicks, but they were able to move past them. They made it to the Eastern Conference Finals for the first time, where they fell again to the Detroit Pistons. The Pistons had emerged as the only answer to Michael Jordan in the league with their "Jordan Rules" (a set of rules that constantly double- and triple-teamed MJ in an effort to tire him out and remove him from the game plan).[51] The front office, never discouraged, would only continue to improve the team.

---

51 Jeff Zillgitt, "'The Last Dance': How the Pistons Employed 'The Jordan Rules' Against Michael Jordan," *USA Today*, April 27, 2020.

PHIL JACKSON AND THE TRIANGLE OFFENSE

Despite yearly improvements in both record and playoff success, Doug Collins' tenure as head coach came to an end after the Eastern Conference Finals (ECF) loss to the Pistons. His hard-nosed approach was not landing like it used to and the Bulls' offense was basically just giving the ball to Jordan. The team needed a new approach. Enter Phil Jackson.

Jackson was a young assistant under Collins but quickly generated respect and buzz around the league. Tex Winter was brought in as his lead assistant and with him, the triangle offense. The triangle offense gives an opportunity to every player on the floor to score; every single cut and screen has a purpose. The offense ebbs and flows depending on the defense.[52] That's about as far as I'm going to dive into it because that's not the point of this book, and I'm neither a coach nor a YouTube "coach" (you know who you are). The point is, everyone on the Bulls had opportunities to score and if the offense stalled, then you could put the ball in the hands of the greatest scorer the NBA has ever seen.

Did the increased opportunities hinder Jordan? Not even close. MJ led the league in scoring for the fourth straight season (33.57 points per game) and was accompanied in the All-Star game by Scottie Pippen for the first time. The system did not make Jordan any worse; it made the rest of the team that much better.

---

52 Dan Barry, "The Triangle Offense, a Simple Yet Perplexing System, Dies," *The New York Times*, June 28, 2017.

This new version of the Bulls was steamrolling teams. They won fifty-five games and faced little opposition in the first two rounds of the playoffs, losing one game in each series. The ball was flying, and everyone was contributing. B.J. Armstrong, a rookie picked up in that year's draft, was an immediate boost to the bench. So, the Bulls would make it to the Eastern Conference Finals again, meet the Pistons again, and they'd lose again. They pushed the Pistons to the brink, forcing a Game 7, but they were blown out in that deciding game. The Bulls simply could not figure that team out.

THE FIRST THREE-PEAT

As with most stars that had not won a ring, talk began that Jordan, for all of his accomplishments, wasn't a winner and couldn't lead a team to a title. However, the Bulls were just getting started. Pippen had introduced himself to the NBA as a legit star the season prior, and he would continue to add to his resume in the 1990–91 season. While Jordan was named to first team All-Defense for the fourth straight season, Scottie was named to the second team for the first time. Jordan, the best two-way player on the planet, had another two-way superstar at his side. There were no big changes to the roster, simply another year of development for the Bulls relatively young roster and another year of integrating the triangle offense.

The 1990–91 season was the year it all came together. The Bulls won sixty-one games, the most wins in franchise history (at the time) and the first time they had ever eclipsed sixty games. They swept the Knicks in the first round of the playoffs and only lost one game (by two points) to the 76ers in the second round. They met the Pistons for the umpteenth time in the ECF. The Pistons had an injury-riddled season, but all of their heavy hitters played in that series. The Bulls swept them. Some, if not all, of their demons were exercised. They met the Los Angeles Lakers in the Finals, an aging but still talented team. The Bulls lost just one game en route to the franchise's (and Jordan's) first title. Michael Jordan was the regular season MVP and the Finals MVP.

The 1991–92 season was more of the same for the Bulls. They made no noticeable changes to the roster, running the championship squad back out. Not only was that squad just as good, they improved. Pippen made an All-NBA team (second), joined MJ on the first team All-Defense, and was a starter on the All-Star team. All for the first time. MJ was the regular season MVP for the second straight year. The team won sixty-seven games, improving their franchise record, and continued their dominance into the playoffs. They swept the Heat in the second round, finished off the Knicks in seven games, and beat the Cavaliers in six.

They met the Blazers in the Finals, the team that had passed on Jordan years ago. Bowie was no longer on the Blazers by this time. However, it was a matchup between Jordan and Drexler, the player who made the Blazers comfortable enough to pass on MJ. Clyde "The Glide" Drexler was having an impressive season himself, joining Jordan as an All-NBA First Team player. Drexler even got the better of MJ in a couple of matchups, stealing the ball from him late in Game 4 to spark a win that evened the series at two apiece. However, Jordan would lead the Bulls and win the next two games, ending the series in six. The Bulls repeated and MJ repeated as both MVP and Finals MVP.

In the 1992–93 season, the Bulls became just the third franchise in NBA history to three-peat as champions (Minneapolis Lakers and Russell Celtics being the other two). Despite winning ten less games than the last season, the Bulls swept the Hawks and the Cavs in the first two rounds. The Knicks, who always put up a fight against the Bulls, took them to six games. They met the Phoenix Suns in the Finals. The Suns actually put up a good fight against the Bulls as Charles Barkley destroyed them on the boards and Kevin Johnson led the series in assists. However, it came down to Jordan setting the Finals record in points per game (41.0) and John Paxson hitting a three in Game 6 with 3.9 seconds left to win by one point. The Bulls had won three straight and it seemed like their only opponent was themselves (foreshadowing alert!).

JORDAN RETIRES! (KIND OF)

Right before the 1993–94 season started; Michael Jordan somewhat surprisingly retired from basketball in the middle of his prime. His father had been murdered three months prior to this, and it weighed heavily into his decision.

"When I lose the sense of motivation and the sense of 'to prove something' as a basketball player, it's time for me to move away from the game of basketball," Jordan told reporters at a press conference announcing his retirement.[53]

He moved on to the game of baseball, as he signed with the Chicago White Sox minor league affiliate. The Bulls would continue to make moves to build their roster, remaining competitive despite losing the best player in the NBA for essentially nothing. Part of this was slotting B.J. Armstrong in MJ's old spot. Steve Kerr was signed to assume the backup guard duties vacated by B.J. With MJ's production needing to be replaced, other players had to step up, and they did.

B.J. Armstrong was an All-Star for the first time. Horace Grant joined him. Pippen, a perennial All-Star, was obviously there and won All-Star MVP.

Fun Fact!

This is the only year in the entirety of this dynasty that the Bulls had three All-Stars; they never did with Jordan!

Scottie Pippen was named to the first team All-NBA for the first time and made first team All-Defense for the third straight year. The Bulls got contributions from several other players like Cartwright, Purdue, and rookie Toni Kukoc.

---

53 "Excerpts of Jordan's Remarks," *The Washington Post*, accessed June 5, 2020.

The Bulls won just two less games than the season prior and swept the Cavaliers in the first round of the playoffs. They would lose to the Knicks in a gritty seven games in the second round though, the Knicks finally getting one on the (Jordan-less) Bulls.

JORDAN RETURNS! (KIND OF)

Despite what the title of this section dictates, the Bulls started the 1994-95 season without MJ. They also started the season without John Paxson (retired), Bill Cartwright (signed with the SuperSonics), and Horace Grant (signed with the Orlando Magic). The front office tried their best to fill the gaps in their roster. They signed Ron Harper (of "Fuck this Bullshit" fame), a defensive minded guard with a sweet midrange game to replace Paxson.[54] Toni Kukoc started in place of Grant, and Will Purdue started in place of Cartwright. The Bulls picked up Jud Buechler (free agency) and traded for Luc Longley to shore up the bench. Despite the pickups, the Bulls were struggling. They had already lost their best player from the three-peat and now they had to replace many of the role players as well. The Bulls limped into the playoffs at 47–35, their worst record in six seasons.

Right before the playoffs, however, the Bulls got their savior back. Michael Jordan, enjoying a solid but unspectacular career in minor league baseball, announced his return

---

54 Jason Owens, "Craig Ehlo 'shocked' by Ron Harper's 'Last Dance' Comments, Doesn't Remember Him 'wanting to play defense'," *Yahoo! Sports*, April 30, 2020.

on March 18. His agent faxed out a release statement on his behalf that simply read:

"I'm back."[55]

MJ played the last seventeen games of the season, looking very much like himself. He scored fifty-five points (dubbed as the "Double Nickel" game) in just his fifth game back against his favorite opponent, the New York Knicks.[56] With Jordan returning to the fold, the Bulls were suddenly much scarier in the playoffs. They beat the Hornets in four games and moved onto the next round: the Orlando Magic. This was a personal matchup; Horace Grant had ditched the Bulls for the up-and-coming Magic in the off-season. Both sides had a point to make. The Bulls challenged Horace to beat them, and they doubled the stars (Shaquille O'Neal and Penny Hardaway) so he would be open. They didn't think he had the stuff, but he did. He averaged eighteen points a game and the Magic knocked off the Bulls in six games.

THE THREE-PEAT SEQUEL

The Bulls started the 1995–96 season with nearly a completely different lineup than the years before. In July, they lost B.J. Armstrong in an expansion draft to the Toronto Raptors. Reports say that B.J. was unhappy with Jordan's return and wanted to move to a contending team that would start him,

---

55 J.A. Adande, "Michael Jordan's Famous 'I'm back' Fax, 25 Years Later," *ESPN*, March 18, 2020.

which could have prompted the Bulls to let him go in the expansion draft. The Bulls were obviously okay with starting MJ at shooting guard and letting Kerr maintain the backup guard duties. Instead, they wanted to address the power forward position. While Kukoc had performed admirably after Grant's departure, there was little depth behind him, and the Bulls wanted to upgrade.

So, the Bulls sent starting center Will Purdue to the Spurs in return for stud power forward Dennis Rodman. Rodman currently led the league in rebounds for four straight seasons and was a tenacious defender. He was also a member of those "Bad Boys" Pistons that eliminated MJ from so many playoffs earlier in his career. Despite concerns about Rodman's "eccentric" lifestyle (I could write another full book on his exploits; if someone has already done so, check it out), the Bulls' management felt that MJ's leadership and fire would be able to keep him in check.[56] Harper, MJ, Pippen, Rodman, and Longley (replaced Purdue) was the new starting lineup. Steve Kerr, Buechler, and Kukoc manned what was quite possibly the best bench in the NBA that year.

The 95–96 Bulls may have had the best season in league history. They became the first team in NBA history to win seventy games, going 72–10. While the Warriors broke that record (73–9) in the 2015–16 season, they were unable to win a championship that season. 72–10 has a better *ring* to it (or so they say). It's also the greatest single season improvement

---

56 Rick Gano, "Bulls Acquire Rodman from Spurs," *The Washington Post*, October 3, 1995.

(47 to 72 wins) in league history. Individual accolades are as follows:

- Jordan and Pippen were both first team All-NBA and All-Star starters.
- Jordan, Pippen, and Rodman were all first team All-Defense. They were just the fifth triplet of teammates to do this in the same season, no one has done it since.
- Toni Kukoc received the Sixth Man of the Year award.
- Phil Jackson received the Coach of the Year award.
- Jerry Krause received the Executive of the Year award.
- Michael Jordan became just the second player in NBA history (Willis Reed of the Knicks did it in 1970) to achieve the "Triple Crown": All-Star MVP, Regular Season MVP, and Finals MVP in the same season.

In the playoffs, they swept the Heat, dropped just one game against the Knicks, and swept the Magic (exacting revenge from the year prior) on their way to the Finals. The matchup was against the Seattle Supersonics and the reigning DPOY Gary Payton. While the series lasted six games, the Bulls built an insurmountable 3–0 lead (no one in NBA history has ever come back from a 3–0 deficit) to begin. Jordan and the Bulls were champions yet again.

The Bulls were back in business and it did not stop in 1996–97. The Bulls added Robert Parish, a Celtics legend and Hall of Famer, but he was far into his twilight by that time. He would provide solid minutes off the bench but was never relied on heavily, think of today's Vince Carter on the Atlanta Hawks (if you're reading this in the future and this no longer tracks, sorry?). The Bulls went 69–13. They lost the last two games of the season, losing the chance to be the first and only team in NBA history to log back-to-back seventy-win seasons. The two-season stretch, including the 72–10 year, remains the best two-season record in NBA history.

In the playoffs, they swept Washington and dropped one game apiece against the Hawks and Heat. They met the legendary Stockton-Malone Jazz in the Finals. The Bulls won the first two games in Chicago, but the Jazz won both in Utah. The series stood at two apiece. Jordan's famous "flu game" occurred in Game 5 of this series in Utah, with MJ dropping thirty-eight points in a narrow two-point win despite experiencing intense flu symptoms (or pizza or a hangover or whatever conspiracy you subscribe to).[57] The Bulls took care of business at home, where they had only lost two games during the regular season. A four-point win aided by a Steve Kerr dagger in the final seconds gave the Bulls their fifth title in seven years. However, turmoil would ensue in the off-season for the back-to-back champions.

The 1997–98 season was tumultuous for the Chicago Bulls, though you wouldn't know it by simply looking at their record. Scottie Pippen needed surgery on his foot and elected to have the surgery right before the season started, as opposed to spending his summer rehabbing. He would miss the first two months of the season. Dennis Rodman was having contract disputes with the team. Michael Jordan, thirty-four years old and nearing the end of his prime, told the team and media that he would retire if Phil Jackson was

---

57   Gabriel Fernandez, "How the Legend of Michael Jordan's 'flu game' Has Evolved Since the 1997 NBA Finals," *CBS Sports*, May 20, 2020.

not the Bulls coach the following season. Jackson himself was having issues with the front office and the relationship seemed unfixable, with GM Jerry Krause announcing that this would be Jackson's last year with the team, championship or not.[58]

Media and opponents alike were reporting issues, real or fake, about the team constantly.

"I can't remember when there has been this many distractions. The only thing might compare is perhaps the year Michael was retired. There was bickering during training camp with Horace Grant. Injuries. Everything seemed to be going wrong. But that does not compare to this," Phil Jackson told reporters before the season.[59]

It seemed that the Bulls dynasty was ending, regardless of the outcome of the season (you could even call it The Last Ballad or something like that).

Regardless of these issues, the team marched on. Despite playing faster and younger teams, the Bulls beat opponents through veteran expertise. MJ, Pippen, Rodman, Harper, and Kerr were all older than thirty-two and yet, the Bulls went 62–20. They swept the Nets and lost just one game to the Hornets. They met the Reggie Miller-led Pacers in the Eastern Conference Finals. This iteration of the Pacers was one of the biggest threats within the Conference to the Bulls

---

58 Mike Wise, "N.B.A. Preview '97-'98: End of Line for Dynasty? Aging Bulls to Face Challenge from Several Teams," *The New York Times*, October 29, 1997.

59 Ibid.

since the "Bad Boys" Pistons that troubled MJ so much earlier in his career. A difficult series where no team won on the road left the Bulls winning in Game 7 by just five points. The Pacers just did not have enough. However, bigger issues loomed ahead.

The Bulls booked a ticket to a rematch with the Jazz. The difference? The Jazz had home court advantage this time and ten days of rest after sweeping the Lakers in the Western Conference Finals. The Bulls had just two days of rest after their grueling series with the Pacers. This discrepancy came to cost the Bulls as they started off slow in Game 1 and faced an early series deficit. It was the first time since their first title that the Bulls dropped Game 1 of the Finals. Behind Jordan's scoring, the Bulls rallied to win the next three games of the series, including a 96–54 embarrassment of the Jazz in Game 3. That game still stands today as the biggest margin of victory in a Finals game in NBA history. The Jazz scrapped together a two-point victory in Game 5 to force a Game 6. The Bulls had yet to go to seven games in any of their championships, and they weren't starting now. With less than twenty seconds on the clock and the Jazz up by one point, Jordan stole the ball from Karl Malone and hit one of the most famous shots in NBA history to win the game by one point. Jordan made the last two plays of the game to win.

It was the sixth championship in eight years for the Bulls and as many Finals MVPs for Jordan. Jordan was again the regular season MVP and All-Star MVP this season, becoming the only player in NBA History to achieve the MVP Triple Crown twice.

DISMANTLING A DYNASTY

The Bulls cleaned house the following off-season. Phil Jackson moved on and Jordan retired (again, kinda) as expected. Buechler and Rodman were both released and signed with other teams. Steve Kerr was traded for Chuck Person and a future first-round pick. Luc Longley was traded for three players that all have career averages of less than ten points a game and a future first-round pick. Finally, Scottie Pippen, MJ's right-hand man and an NBA superstar himself, was traded for a player who was cut by the team a season later and a future second-round pick. The team was old and moving on was not necessarily a bad idea, but what the Bulls got back in return was next to nothing. A disaster.

Jerry Krause, the man who built and sustained this dynasty, was well out of his depth in dealing with the next stage of the organization. He would last as the general manager for five seasons following the Bulls' championships. The team surpassed twenty wins just once in that stretch.

The Bulls dominated for nearly a decade, and they would spend the next decade and a half mired in mediocrity.

FINAL THOUGHTS

The Chicago Bulls did something rare at the time for competing teams. They realized the talent they had right away and decided to build around it, even if they received some backlash from veteran players. They achieved real success with Doug Collins but were still able to make the difficult decision of firing him in favor of Phil Jackson, who took the Bulls to another stratosphere. Jackson and Tex Winter (much like Auerbach with the fast break) introduced a new aspect to the game of basketball in the triangle offense that would revolutionize the game.

The Bulls also nailed their draft picks, another necessity thus far for dynasties. Lastly, it was the continued desire of adding talent to the roster that helped, especially in the second three-peat. Every time the Bulls lost a player, they made sure to replace them right away with someone of equal or better value. The Bulls may have had the (arguably) greatest player of all time, but they ensured that he was surrounded by a real supporting cast for much of his career.

Looking at the formula, we're averaging the scores from their first title in 1991 up until their final title in 1998. That eight-year average comes out to a Dynasty Score of 19.163. That is the second highest average out of the dynasties we look at. If you take out the two Jordan-less seasons in the middle, the score is still second at 20.64, so please do not come for me Jordan stans.

What the Bulls dynasty does own is the highest single season Dynasty Score with their monumental 72–10-win season in 1996 (25.875). Phil Jackson was a key reserve for the New York Knicks' title run in 1973, so he qualified as a Proven Winner for the entirety of the run. What set the Bulls apart in the formula was in their drafting and their defense. Yes, Jordan and Pippen were top ten lottery picks, but they always made shrewd trades to be in those draft positions. They also hit on some non-lottery picks, like

BJ Armstrong at eighteenth overall. The Bulls were the only team to have three players on an All-Defensive team in a season (out of the teams we examine) and they had it twice. For the seventy-two-win season, Jordan won the MVP, Phil Jackson won the Coach of the Year, and Toni Kukoc won the Sixth Man of the Year Award. They raked in points for that.

Fun Fact!

In the 1999 draft, the Chicago Bulls drafted Elton Brand with the first overall pick and Metta World Peace with the sixteenth overall pick. Both players were traded within two seasons of the draft and they both became All-Stars after leaving Chicago.

EPILOGUE: MR. JORDAN GOES TO WASHINGTON

JUST KIDDING, see you in the next chapter. :)

CHAPTER 5:

THE SECOND COMING
OF SHOWTIME

FOREWORD:

This chapter was originally written before Kobe Bryant's (along with his daughter and seven other passengers) devastating, untimely, and tragic death. I wanted to write a foreword to this chapter to address this and also Kobe's public Colorado scandal in 2003. It is not necessarily nice to bring up, but I felt that it is still important, so here are the full, unbiased facts:

- Kobe Bryant was arrested on July 2, 2003 in relation to a sexual assault case, a hotel employee had accused him of raping her.
- He was acquitted on September 1, 2004 because the accuser refused to testify.
- On the same day, Kobe delivered a public apology to the accuser during a live press conference.

- In August 2004, the accuser brought a civil suit against Kobe Bryant, which they settled out of court.[60]

That's it. That's what happened. I'm not going to make any comments on the validity of the accusations or the accuser. It is up to your interpretation. Feel free to research it further if you are interested. Beyond this incident, Kobe Bryant was nothing but one of the best competitors of all time, and seemingly a fantastic father. Let's move onto the chapter.

While Jordan's Bulls were in the midst of their second three-peat, the next dynasty was brewing in the Western Conference. The Lakers have the all-time NBA record with thirty-one Finals appearances. They have sixteen championships, which is the second most all time (Celtics have seventeen). Their latest run was with Kobe Bryant, but the dynasty part of that iteration (a three-peat) was with both Kobe and Shaquille O'Neal. It continued the tradition of all-time big men on the Lakers, and the Kobe-Shaq combo instilled nostalgia of the Magic-Kareem era of the '80s. It was indeed a return to Showtime for the Lakers, and it began in the 1996 off-season.

OFF-SEASON HEISTS

Jerry West, a familiar face in both Lakers and dynasty history, was running the team in the 1996 off-season, which started off bittersweet. Magic Johnson announced his retirement

---

60 Kevin Draper, "Kobe Bryant and the Sexual Assault Case That Was Dropped but Not Forgotten," *The New York Times*, January 27, 2020.

after thirteen glorious seasons. The retirement was the only bitter part of the off-season though, as West pulled off a series of moves that have been unrivaled since. It started with trading Vlade Divac, the Lakers starter at center for six straight seasons, for the thirteenth pick in the draft. They took Kobe Bryant in that spot. Jerry West had his eyes on the young prospect for the entire year. Kobe's pre-draft workout with the Lakers has become the stuff of legends. Jerry West had him play one-on-one with Michael Cooper, the former defensive player of the year who played for the Showtime dynasty. Cooper was older now, but he could still get the better of inexperienced players—but not Kobe. West called off the training early saying:

"Best workout I've ever seen. He's better than anybody we have on the team right now. Let's go."[61]

The Lakers used their original spot in the draft, the twenty-fourth pick, to select Derek Fischer. He would be a massive part of their dynasty run as well. Then came the big man.

They stole Shaquille O'Neal, a 7'1", 250-pound behemoth, in free agency from the Orlando Magic. "Diesel" was the most dominant big man in the NBA at the time. O'Neal had been low-balled by the Magic and desired to take his glowing personality to Hollywood. On his decision, Shaq had this to say:

"Jerry West is the reason I came to the Lakers."[62]

---

61 Kevin Ding, "Kobe Bryant's Predraft Workout Has Become Stuff of Lakers, and NBA, Legend," *Bleacher Report*, June 24, 2014.

62 Roland Lazenby, *Showboat: The Life of Kobe Bryant* (New York: Back Bay Books, 2016), 353.

The team started fast. Shaq was as advertised, averaging twenty-six points and twelve rebounds with nearly three blocks per game. However, Jerry West was not content. In January of that year, he sent Cedric Ceballos and Rumeal Robinson to the Phoenix Suns and received Robert Horry among smaller pieces in return. Horry's stats didn't pop off the page, but he was a Proven Winner (went back to back with the Rockets in '94 and '95) and is considered one of the clutch-est players of all time. So, in one off-season, West compiled three of the starters and one of the best closers of their championship run in one year. The man knows his shit.

The team finished 56–26, which was their most wins in six seasons. They did this despite Shaq, who was always banged up, missing thirty-one games. He was still named to the All-Star game (missed due to injury) and the All-NBA third team. Eddie Jones, a defensive-minded small forward, was also named to the All-Star game. Kobe, meanwhile, was named to the All-Rookie second team. The Lakers entered the playoffs second in their division. They beat the Portland Trail Blazers 3–1, no contest. They then met the juggernaut Utah Jazz (who ruled the Western Conference in the early '90s, but always lost to MJ and the Bulls in the Finals), where they would only win one game. In Game 2, a two-point loss, Robert Horry went 7–7 from three, which remains a record for three-point makes with no misses in a playoff game. The Lakers were on the rise, and there was more help on the way.

The 1997–98 season showed that the Lakers were truly a rising giant, and not just a fun young team. West signed Rick Fox in the off-season, a solid player whose impact went beyond the box score. He could score and board, but he was a great team leader and an iron man, playing and starting in all eighty-two games that first season with the Lakers. The team started 11–0, the best start in franchise history.

They were a young team through and through, the only team in the league that year without a player thirty-plus years old. Shaq again would miss time. He missed twenty games. His absence meant that someone else would have to carry the scoring burden, and in came Kobe "Black Mamba" Bryant. Kobe brought an electric scoring off the bench and he was rewarded by becoming the youngest All-Star in NBA history. He only started one game that year, the least by an All-Star ever. Shaq, Eddie Jones, and Nick Van Exel joined him as All-Stars. It was the first time in fifteen years that a team had four All-Stars, and it still has only happened eight times. Shaq led the league in field goal percentage (while also being near the bottom of the league in free throw percentage which, congrats) and was named to the All-NBA first team. Eddie Jones was named to the All-Defense second team.

The Lakers dominated the early rounds of the playoffs. Again, they beat the Blazers in the first round, dropping just one game. They met the Seattle Supersonics in the second round, again losing just one game. This was the first time they had reached the Western Conference Finals in seven seasons. The trip did not last long. They, again, went against the Utah Jazz. The Lakers were swept. Karl Malone was a monster and the Lakers had trouble guarding All-Star caliber power forwards, of which the Western Conference was home to many. West would focus on this issue in the next season.

LOCKOUT SEASON

The 1998–99 season did not begin until February 5, a result of long negotiations for a new Collective Bargaining Agreement between the NBA and the NBPA. Once the new CBA was agreed upon, the season began. Because the season started this late, there was no All-Star game.[63] In the midst of the discussions, Michael Jordan announced his second retirement from the NBA. It was the last time he would play in a Bulls jersey. Jordan's retirement meant one thing: the league was wide open. Half the league believed they had a chance to win the title now, including the Lakers.

Soon after the shortened fifty-game season began, Jerry West signed Dennis Rodman. Rodman, who you recognize from the previous dynasty, was exactly the defensive power forward the Lakers needed. About two weeks later, the Lakers traded Elden Campbell and Eddie Jones for Glen Rice, J.R. Reid, and B.J. Armstrong (also from the Bulls dynasty). Rice was an All-Star and an incredible scorer on the wing. The Lakers adding two members of the previous dynasty was the last piece of the puzzle, right? Wrong.

They waived Armstrong immediately after the trade and did the same with Rodman, amid several off-season issues (good ol' Rodzilla), a few weeks later. They traded Nick Van Exel for Tyronn Lue and end-of-bench players. Lue would serve as a very solid backup point guard for the Lakers (when he wasn't getting stepped over by Allen Iverson). Head Coach

---

63 Thomas Golianopoulos, "'An Unmitigated Disaster': An Oral History of the Lockout-Shortened 1999 NBA Season," *The Ringer*, February 19, 2019.

Del Harris was fired in the midst of a three-game losing streak and was replaced with assistant Kurt Rambis (remember him?). Shaq made second team All-NBA and Kobe, in his first season as a starter, made third team. The team made quick work of the first round again, dropping one game to the Houston Rockets. As was tradition though, the Lakers would get walloped by the team that would eventually make the Finals. They were swept by the Spurs, who would go on to win the title.

FAMILIAR FACES INSPIRE A TITLE RUN

Jerry West was reportedly content with handing the full-time head coaching reigns over to Kurt Rambis, who had won titles with the Showtime Lakers. The Lakers fans, however, who have always chased big names (for better or for 2013 Dwight Howard), demanded someone with more pedigree. So, the Lakers brought Phil Jackson, the "Zen Master," on board.

This was a member from the Bulls dynasty that would pan out (honestly kind of upset that Jackson wasn't here a year earlier, probably could have kept Rodman in check). He brought Tex Winter back as his lead assistant. Apparently, the Lakers were feeling nostalgic, as they added another member from the Bulls dynasty (Ron Harper) and a member from the previous Lakers dynasty (A.C. Green) to the roster. The once baby Lakers suddenly had a plethora of Proven Winners and seasoned veterans. A.C Green in particular, was thirty-six and started every game that year.

The veteran presence mixed with young stars had fantastic results. The team went 67–15, the second-best record in franchise history. Shaq's 1999–2000 season was possibly the best season of his career:

- Regular season MVP
- Scoring crown (29.67 points per game)
- First Team All-NBA
- Second Team All-Defense
- All-Star MVP

Kobe blossomed into a star this season as well. He was named to the second team All-NBA and became the youngest player in league history to be named first team All-Defense. The Lakers went into the playoffs red-hot but had more trouble than usual in the first round. They won a winner-takes-all Game 6 against the Kings and then dropped just one game against the Suns. They advanced to the Western Conference Finals against one of their favorite punching bags: the Trail Blazers.

This time, the Blazers had counters to the punches. They pushed the Lakers to another deciding game, but the Lakers pulled out a five-point victory in Game 7 to advance to the Finals. There they met the Reggie Miller-led Pacers, known as one of the bigger threats to MJ's reign a couple years prior. They were still dangerous. They actually forty-balled (beat them by forty plus points, please keep up) the Lakers in Game 5, but Shaq (forty-one points) and company took care of business in a five-point Game 6 series clincher. The Lakers were champions for the first time since the '80s. Shaq was named the Finals MVP and became just the third player in NBA history to secure the NBA "Triple Crown" (Jordan and Reed).

Just because the Lakers won the title didn't mean that they were content with the current roster. After losing a power struggle with Phil Jackson (never was one to have good relationships with management), Jerry West resigned from his position. He was replaced with Mitch Kupchak (remember him, part two). Early in the 2000–01 season, the Lakers engaged in a massive four-team trade. Here's basically what the Lakers gave up and what they got back:

- Gave up: Glen Rice, first round pick, end-of-bench players
- Got back: Greg Foster, Horace Grant, end-of-bench players
    - Note: Luc Longley was part of this trade with two non-Lakers teams, just wanted to mention him because nostalgia and the Bulls and dynasties and whatnot.

Foster served as a solid backup center to Shaq, even starting for him when he would miss time. Horace Grant (yet another Bulls championship member) was the Lakers' starting power forward. He, as proven in other title runs, could score and was an accomplished defender at the position. A.C. Green signed with Miami, giving the starting small forward spot back to Rick Fox. The Lakers once again had injuries to several key members of the team, including Kobe, Shaq, and Derek Fischer. Fischer in particular, missed over sixty games. The Lakers survived through the depth that they had acquired. Ron Harper, Tyronn Lue, and Greg Foster all made starts in place of those injuries. Brian Shaw, who had been signed in the previous off-season, made key starts for Kobe.

The depth stayed the course and the Lakers were able to finish 56–26, making them first in the Pacific Division. With all of their stars healthy for the playoffs, the Lakers embarked on one of the most dominant playoff runs in league history. They swept the Trail Blazers (poor guys) in the first round, swept the Kings in the second round, and swept the Spurs (revenge for years prior) in the Conference Finals. They met the Allen Iverson-led 76ers in the Finals. The Lakers lost the first game of the series but won the next four (this has been called a "douchebag sweep" by some, which I think is hilarious and should be used more often) en route to their second straight title. This team held the record for win percentage in the playoffs (.938) until the Golden State Warriors bested it in 2017.

Shaq was awarded the Finals MVP, which added to another season full of accolades for the big man. Kobe was second team All-Defense (Shaq joined him on that roster this year) and second team All-NBA. The team was riding high but would have to fill several open spots on the roster in the off-season.

For the second straight off-season, the Lakers lost key contributors to their championship team. Ron Harper retired after a storied career with two different championship franchises. Tyronn Lue and Horace Grant both left in free agency. The Lakers needed to replace their starting power forward and two guard positions. They started by trading Greg Foster to the Milwaukee Bucks for Lindsey Hunter, a seasoned veteran guard who would end up starting half the season for the Lakers as injuries again piled up.

The Lakers then signed two forwards in free agency, Mitch Richmond and Samaki Walker. Walker was a solid all-around player that could play either forward spot and even started for an injured Shaq a couple times (Walker was a wildly inconsistent player but gave the Lakers good minutes from time to time). Richmond was a seasoned veteran who was, at one point, a six-time All-Star. He only played spot minutes but was one of those vets that every contending team needs. The depth would be needed as Shaq and Derek Fischer would miss extended time again.

Despite injuries and roster turnover, the Lakers won two more games in the 2001–02 season than they did in the previous year. Shaq and Kobe became the first teammates since MJ and Scottie Pippen to be named to the All-NBA first team. Shaq led the league in field goal percentage for the fifth straight season (57.93 percent), something that has only been accomplished by two other players. Kobe was again in the All-Star game without Shaq (injured) and this time he would walk away with the All-Star MVP. With this success, they marched into the playoffs.

They met the Trail Blazers again in the first round and again swept them. They only lost one game to the Spurs in the next round, moving on to the Western Conference Finals. The next round is the only series that challenged the Lakers that postseason and it is one of most controversial series in NBA history.

Several questionable calls happened throughout the series and the Tim Donaghy scandal followed.

Exposition time!

Basically, Tim Donaghy was caught gambling on the games he was refereeing and some think (still no evidence) that his gambling heavily influenced this specific series.[64]

They were well on their way to a 3–1 deficit had Robert "Big Shot Bob" Horry had not hit a three at the buzzer to win Game 4. The teams traded victories after that game and it went to a deciding Game 7 in Sacramento, where the Lakers won in overtime. People will call attention to the questionable calls, but it does not help the Kings' case that they were 16–30 at the free throw line and 2–30 from three. After the scandal broke, Kings' coach, Rick Adelman, had this to say to reporters:

"My first thought [upon hearing Donaghy's allegation] was: I knew it. I'm not going to say there was a conspiracy. I just think something wasn't right. It was unfair. We didn't have a chance to win that game."[65]

This was the first time in franchise history that the Lakers won a Game 7 on the road. They booked a ticket against the Jason Kidd-led Nets, whom they swept easily. The Lakers had themselves a three-peat and Shaq became the second

---

64 Chris Sheridan, "2002 Lakers-Kings Game 6 at Heart of Donaghy allegations," *ESPN*, June 10, 2008.

65 Ibid.

player in NBA history to win three straight Finals MVPs (Jordan).

FOUR-PEAT FALLS SHORT

In the off-season, the Lakers traded Lindsey Hunter to the Toronto Raptors for two bench players that would play barely fifteen minutes combined per game and a future second-round pick. Beyond that, the team basically ran it back with the same championship roster as the previous year. It was a rough year for them, as they started 11–19. This was their worst start in thirty years. The slow start was mainly due to Shaq missing fifteen games, basically an annual tradition at this point.

Despite the slow start and the injuries, the Lakers finished a respectable 50–32. Kobe was nearing his peak this season, earning first team bids to both the All-NBA team and the All-Defense team. Shaq joined him on the first team All-NBA but was second team All-Defense. The Lakers were back in the playoffs and were primed to make another run.

They beat the Timberwolves in six games, but the injury bug finally bit them in the playoffs. Iron man Rick Fox tore a ligament in his foot during the series and was out for the playoffs. The injury and growing chemistry issues (foreshadowing alert!) led to a loss in six games to the Spurs (who would go on to win the title).

THE SUPERTEAM IS BORN

Some people blame the Warriors for the rise of "superteams" in recent years, after they added Kevin Durant to an already exceptional team. Some people blame the Miami Heat (brought LeBron and Chris Bosh to join Dwyane Wade) for giving them the idea. Wait until you hear what the 2003–04 Lakers did. The Lakers brought Horace Grant back into the fold. Then, they signed Karl Malone and Gary Payton, two of the most dominant players of the decade. They signed for much cheaper than what they were worth. Payton explained that decision in an interview years later:

"Karl and I had taken a pay cut to play with these guys. We weren't into that anymore. I was into going somewhere and winning multiple championships."[66]

They may have been in the later years of their careers but between the two they had:

- Twenty-three All-Star appearances
- Twenty-three All-NBA team bids
- Thirteen All-Defense bids
- Two MVP awards
- One Defensive Player of the Year award

Suffice to say, the Lakers were going all in for at least one more title. These new pieces wouldn't harm Shaq and Kobe's production, as they both made first team All-NBA. Shaq was

---

66   Ric Bucher, "An Oral History of the 2003-04 Los Angeles Lakers, the 1st Super Team," *Bleacher Report*, May 26, 2015.

named the All-Star game MVP and again lead the league in field goal percentage (58.4 percent) after being edged out the season before. They were very heavy favorites to win the title. But trouble was brewing.

Kobe and Shaq had a public feud that wasn't a major issue until this season. Kobe, who trained like a man possessed, wanted Shaq to take his training and health more seriously. He felt that Shaq's annual missed time was hurting the team. Shaq, always the fun-loving, compassionate man, fully disagreed. They would have many back-and-forths during the season, such as Kobe telling reporters:

"Scoring shouldn't affect [O'Neal's] defense."[67]

Shaq retaliated with the following:

"If the big dog ain't me, then the house won't get guarded—period."[68]

They would both miss fifteen plus games that season. Karl Malone himself missed half the season with injuries. Gary Payton struggled to adapt to the triangle offense and spent much of the season underperforming. Kobe himself had a very public scandal in Colorado and would miss games for his trial.

The issues didn't seem to plague them in the early rounds of the playoffs. They dropped just one game to the Rockets,

---

67 Mike Wise, "PRO BASKETBALL; Tension Between O'Neal and Bryant Is Rising Every Day," *The New York Times*, January 11, 2001.

68 Ibid.

got revenge on the Spurs in six games, and beat the Timberwolves in six games. They entered the Finals with a matchup against the Detroit Pistons. The Pistons did not have a superstar, but every single player on their roster was a dominant defender and could hit shots. They played like a team, something that this year's Lakers was not too keen on doing.

The Lakers entered as massive favorites and it led to massive disappointment. Tempers flared, injuries lagged key contributors, and the Lakers lost in five games. The games weren't necessarily close either. The team, compiled of several of the most iconic players in NBA history, fell to a scrappy team that dedicated itself to team offense and ferocious defense. Pistons President Joe Dumars summed it up perfectly after the series:

"I knew that they had the two best players in the world, but this is not a tennis match, it is basketball. We did it the right way—working hard, working together."[69]

THE FALL

This loss seemingly killed the Lakers. The feud between Shaq and Kobe boiled over and ended with Shaquille O'Neal requesting, and being granted, a trade to the Miami Heat. The Lakers received Caron Butler, Lamar Odom, and a first back. It is unclear whether Phil Jackson was fired or resigned, but what is clear is he did not leave on good

---

69 Perry A. Farrell, *Tales from the Detroit Pistons Locker Room*, (Illinois: Sports Publishing LLC), 2004, 184.

terms. He would write and publish a book where he tore Kobe apart soon after his departure from the franchise. Horace Grant retired, and Karl Malone would never play another game in the NBA. The Lakers traded Gary Payton and Rick Fox for an ensemble of players that did not pan out. The dynasty was dead.

FINAL THOUGHTS

The "Second Coming of Showtime" had more similarities than just being a fun Lakers team. The dynasty got jump started by the acquisition of an all-time center (Kareem/Shaq), drafted a young tenacious guard to compliment said center (Magic/Kobe), and made sure to keep talent around the roster. This dynasty also introduces "Dynasty DNA": members of former dynasties being brought into the fold and teaching their winning ways to the new group of guys. In this instance, the Lakers brought in Ron Harper (Bulls), Horace Grant (Bulls), and A.C. Green (OG Showtime) knowing that they would be steady and calm when the big games came.

Even more importantly, they hired Phil Jackson, coach of the previous dynasty in Chicago, to head the team. His experience in managing egos from the previous regime was instrumental in the Lakers keeping Kobe and Shaq together as long as they did. We are going to see a lot more "Dynasty DNA" guys in the upcoming chapters. It also helps that Jerry West, who has had his hand in now two dynasties, was calling most of the shots.

Looking at the formula, we are taking the average from their first title in 2000, up until their Finals appearance in 2004. Their best year was the 2001 title, where Shaq won the MVP (DS = 21.875). Their greatest two assets were their stars and their veterans. Their two stars (Kobe and Shaq) racked up All-NBA and All-Defense selections like only the Bulls and the Warriors.

What the Lakers did was surround them with players that knew how to win. These Lakers had at least one "Dynasty DNA" member in each run after their 2000 title. In 2001, they had three of them in Phil Jackson, Ron Harper, and Horace Grant. The learning curve for Shaq and Kobe was much easier due to this veteran presence.

Where this dynasty fell a bit short was a lack of support for Shaq and Kobe. Guys like Derek Fischer, Robert Horry, and Rick Fox are fantastic role players in NBA history and have each had great moments on the greatest stage. The difference is that they relied on Shaq and Kobe to draw attention away from them. Very rarely could they pull it together if the stars were not playing well. Not once during the run did the Lakers have a non-Kobe or Shaq All-Star, All-Defense, or All-NBA player. Their average for the five-season stretch is 18.525, above the OG Showtime Lakers but no one else that we examined.

EPILOGUE

Two seasons later, the Miami Heat won the NBA championship. They were led by Shaq and his new star shooting guard teammate Dwyane Wade. The Lakers would not win a playoff series for four seasons. In 2008–09 the Lakers won the title again. Kobe, Derek Fischer, and (funnily enough) Phil Jackson were the only members of the previous dynasty that were a part of this championship core. Lamar Odom, acquired in the Shaq trade, was essential in that title run. They went back-to-back the following year with the same core. They have two playoff series wins since. Next up is the dynasty of the undead: the San Antonio Spurs.

CHAPTER 6:

THE BIG FUNDAMENTAL AND HIS SPURS

———

The San Antonio Spurs. The gold standard of winning in the NBA. Do they have the most championships in NBA history? Nope. Do they have the most storied and glorious history in the NBA? Not really. But if we're talking winning, especially sustained winning, we're talking the San Antonio Spurs.

They have made the playoffs (at the time of this writing) for twenty-two straight seasons. That's tied with the 76ers who did it from 1950 to 1971.

Fun Fact!

The 76ers went 9–73 the year after making it twenty-two straight, widely regarded as the worst team in NBA history.

In addition to making the playoffs for twenty-two straight seasons, all twenty-two of them have been winning seasons. No one else has had more than twenty straight winning seasons.

For reference, I am twenty-two years old (again, as I am writing this). If I had been born in San Antonio (they would be my team as the laws of being born in locations go), I never would have seen a losing season. As a fan of the Milwaukee Bucks, that sounds impossible (yeah, I know they're good now, get off my back). Their legendary run began in the 1997–98 season. We are going to start a year before that, which coincidentally was their worst season in franchise history.

STARTING LOW(ISH)

Okay, the Spurs got lucky. They are the model of a fantastic front office and they never would have won so much without the incredible draft picks and off-season moves that they conducted year after year. Their run started, however, because of some unluckiness that turned into the ultimate luck. I know that's confusing, but bear with me.

Prior to the 1996–97 season, the Spurs were already a borderline contender in the NBA. They had made the playoffs for seven straight seasons and had one of the best players in the NBA in David "The Admiral" Robinson.

> **Fun Fact!**
> He got that nickname because he served in the Navy prior to his NBA career. He remains the only NBA player who played at the Naval Academy.

Robinson was the DPOY in 1992 and the league MVP in 1995. So, how could 1996–97 be the Spurs franchise's worst season?

The Admiral went down. He broke his foot and only played in six games. The Spurs went 20–62—the unluckiness. Then, they got the number one pick in the draft lottery—the luckiness. Despite injuries being the reason that the team was bad, the Spurs still fired Head Coach Bob Hill eighteen games into the season. He was replaced by Gregg Popovich, who was already the team's general manager at that point. The Spurs took Tim Duncan with the first pick in the draft, and they have not missed the playoffs since.

The 1997–98 season signaled a new era for the Spurs, dubbed the "Twin Towers" era. The Twin Towers were Tim Duncan and David Robinson, who made up one of the best front-court duos in NBA history. Robinson came back from his injury with a vengeance and was named to the All-Defense Second Team and the All-NBA Second Team. Tim Duncan wasn't slacking either. In fact, he outperformed Robinson that season en route to one of the best rookie seasons in league history. A list of his rookie year notables follows:

- Averaged 21.1 points, 11.1 rebounds, 2.5 blocks per game
- All-Star

- Second Team All-Defense
- First Team All-NBA (first rookie since Larry Bird)
- Rookie of the Year

It was clear that the Spurs had struck gold. Other people were taking notice as well. Charles Barkley (one of the best power forwards of that time and all time) had this to say about Tim Duncan after playing him in the All-Star game:

"I have seen the future and he wears number 21."[70]

The Spurs finished the season 56–26. They won their first series against the Phoenix Suns fairly easily and then got whooped 4–1 by the Utah Jazz. Despite the loss, the Spurs were on the rise.

CHAMPIONSHIP SEASON

The 1998–99 season was, as we've already covered, shortened by the lockout. Entering the season, the Spurs wanted to surround their "Twin Towers" with some more shooting. So, they signed Mario Elie, a veteran sniper, to be their starting shooting guard. They also traded for Steve Kerr (remember him?) to back up Elie and starting point guard Avery Johnson. The Spurs went 37–13 and were first in their division.

The Spurs massacred the playoffs. They dropped just one game to the Timberwolves in the first round. They swept

---

70 Ethan Back, "Tim Duncan: The San Antonio Spurs Superstar Will Never Get the Props He Deserves," *Bleacher Report*, January 22, 2011.

the Lakers (who were about to unleash their own dynasty) in the second round. They swept Portland in the Conference Finals. (Man, it seems like every chapter I talk about Portland getting crushed in a decisive series. Sorry guys.) They punched their ticket to the NBA Finals for the first time in Spurs history. There they would meet the New York Knicks, who were the first eight seed to make the Finals in league history. The Spurs paid respect to that milestone by letting them win one game and beating them in five.

The Spurs were champions for the first time in franchise history. The Twin Towers put their stamp on the league and Tim Duncan was named Finals MVP in just his second season. Steve Kerr (and Will Purdue, who they had gotten in the Dennis Rodman trade) were champions again.

Fun Fact!

Steve Kerr remains the only player in the modern era to win four straight titles.

After the season, the Spurs selected Emanuel "Manu" Ginobili (I'm Argentinian so best believe I'm a Manu stan) in the second round of the draft, though he wouldn't come from overseas until 2002.

> **Exposition Time!**
> NBA teams can draft international players if they currently reside outside of the United States and have not played college basketball in the states. International players will sometimes prefer to stay on their team and not go immediately to the NBA after being drafted. Once they do decide to make the jump, they go to the team who drafted them, as they own their draft rights. These rights can be traded or renounced, giving them some value.[71]

RETOOLING SEASONS

Sadly, 1999–2000 was a lost season. The Spurs looked unbeatable. Then, in the last month or so of the season, Duncan went down with a knee injury. The Spurs finished second in their division and lost to Phoenix in the first round. Despite the injury, Duncan was named First Team All-NBA for the third straight season, First Team All-Defense for the second year in a row and was the All-Star game MVP. By this time, Duncan had earned the nickname "The Big Fundamental."

Byron Scott, who was a member of the Lakers dynasty and has coached in the NBA since, sums up the nickname better than I ever could:

---

71 Tom Ziller, "A Complete Primer on Drafting International NBA Prospects," *SBNATION*, June 25, 2014.

"He's not throwing behind-the-back passes, he's not doing tomahawk jams, he's not doing anything that's very flashy. He's just a very unassuming guy who goes about his job, and the next thing you know he's got 23 points and 20 rebounds."[72]

Robinson, thirty-four, was named to the All-Star game and was Third Team All-NBA. For the next two seasons, the Spurs would dominate the regular season but run into the dynasty buzz saw in the playoffs.

In 2000–01, they went 58–24 and were first in their division. Duncan had the same accolades as the season before, minus All-Star MVP. Robinson repeated his accolades. The Spurs lost one game each in the first two series against the Timberwolves and the Mavericks. They were coasting. Then they were swept by the Lakers, who would go on to win the third of their three straight titles. The team drafted Tony Parker from France as twenty-eighth overall in the off-season.

The Spurs made several roster changes before the 2001–02 season. They traded Steve Kerr, a pick, and some end-of-bench players, for Steve Smith (a veteran shooter). They also signed Stephen Jackson, a scorer. The big get was signing Bruce Bowen, an All-Defense player that was in the middle of his prime.

Despite all these changes, this season was more of the same for the Spurs. They again went 58–24. They again were first in their division. Duncan was again first team for both

---

72 Jack McCallum, "The Big Fundamental to Prevail in the Championship Series, the Nets Will Have to Exploit Flaws in the Game of Spurs Star Tim Duncan—If They Can Find Any," *Sports Illustrated*, June 9, 2003.

All-NBA and All-Defense, he was also named the league MVP. Tony Parker was named to the All-Rookie First Team. Bruce Bowen was Second Team All-Defense. They met the Supersonics in the first round and beat them in a competitive series. Then they got crushed by the Lakers again.

END OF AN ERA, BEGINNING OF A NEW ONE

The 2002–03 season could not have been more magical or perfect if it had been written for a movie. It began with David Robinson announcing that this would be his final season— one last stand for the Admiral and his Spurs. So, the team prepared to go for it.

They started with trading for Kerr (again). Ginobili came from overseas to bolster their bench. R.C. Buford was promoted to general manager, allowing Popovich to concentrate fully on coaching. The Spurs moved into a new arena. They went 60–22, first in the division. Manu is named to Second Team All-Rookie. Bruce Bowen was again Second Team All-Defense. Popovich won Coach of the Year, his transition a success. Duncan was the back-to-back regular season MVP, All-NBA First Team, and All-Defense First Team.

The Spurs met Phoenix in the first round, beating them in six games. In the next round, it was a matchup with the Lakers, the team that had bullied them for the past two seasons. They finished them off in six as well. They beat the Mavericks in six to meet the New Jersey Nets who... they beat in six (I don't know if there's any symbolism to add to that but it's kind of fun, no?). Tim Duncan, who was the leading rebounder in every game of that championship series, was again the Finals MVP, and David Robinson went into retirement with another ring. Robinson was elated during the post-game press conference:

"My last game, streamers flying, world champions. How could you write a better script than this?"[73]

POST ROBINSON LIFE

Kerr retired along with Robinson, so the Spurs had some holes to fill. They also lost longtime bench players Jaren Jackson and Speedy Claxton. They brought in Robert Horry (Lakers dynasty member), Rasho Nesterovic (who replaced DR as the starting center), and Hedo Turkoglu (sniper forward) to fill the gaps. The team started off slowly, clearly struggling with the loss of Robinson.

The Spurs went 57–25 and were second in their division (which for them, I guess means they struggled). They swept Memphis in the first round but would again lose to the Lakers in the second round. They had trouble containing Shaquille O'Neal even with Robinson, and simply couldn't stop him without. Derrick Fischer hit a buzzer beater against them in Game 5 that effectively broke their spirit for that postseason.

Buford got to work on improving the roster after a frustrating season. He signed Brent Barry, an all-time three-point

---

73 NBA.com Staff, "Top Moments: Twin Towers Ride Off to Sunset with Another Title," *NBA History*, Accessed June 4, 2020.

shooter, to be their new starting shooting guard. He resigned Manu to a three-year contract. They went 59–23 and were back at the top of the division. They would have easily broken sixty wins that year had Duncan not gotten injured down the stretch. In April, the team signed veteran small forward Glenn Robinson off the buyout market to prepare for the stretch run.

Exposition Time!

The buyout market is a way for contending teams to stock up on players for the stretch run. Toward the end of the season, teams that are out of the playoff picture will usually grant a veteran player's desire to compete in the postseason. These are veterans that are past their primes (but still valuable players) and whose contract is expiring that year (usually). Contending teams will then offer that player a one-year minimum contract to finish the season on their team. It is a good way to add pieces to a roster without needing to trade any of your players. It is also a fun microcosm of capitalism (*woohoo*).[74]

All that mattered, though, was that "The Big Fundamental" would be healthy for the playoffs—and he was.

The Spurs dropped just one game against the Nuggets, beat the Supersonics in six games, and again dropped just one game to the Phoenix Suns. They made it to the Finals fairly

---

74 Sam Quinn, "2020 NBA Buyout Market: How Midseason Free Agency Works, and Who Could Be Available After the Trade Deadline," *CBS Sports*, February 26, 2020.

easily. There they met the Detroit Pistons, a band of gritty defenders who had taken down the Lakers' superteam in the previous season. The Spurs won the first two games but lost by a combined forty-eight points in Game 4 and Game 5. Game 5 came down to overtime and losing three straight to the Pistons, which could spell doom. Robert "Big Shot Bob" Horry hit a three to win by one point (dude always lived up to the moment). They lost Game 6 in Detroit but were able to wrap up the title at home in Game 7. The Spurs were champs again. Here is a list of the team's accolades that year:

- Tim Duncan: First Team All-NBA, First Team All-Defense, Finals MVP (only the fourth player to win this award three times)
- Bruce Bowen: First Team All-Defense
- Manu Ginobili: All-Star

Glenn Robinson left after the title, but that was all the Spurs lost before the 2005–06 season. They added Nick Van Exel (veteran backup point guard) and Michael Finley (veteran shooter off the bench) in free agency to reinforce the team's depth. This was the season that Tony Parker blossomed into a star. He was named to the All-Star team for the first time. He averaged nearly nineteen points a game and just under six assists a game. The Spurs had scored on a late first-round pick. They won sixty-three games, which was a franchise record at the time (the 2015–16 Spurs won sixty-seven games). They beat the Sacramento Kings in the first round, winning in six games. Then, they were shocked by the fourth seed Dallas Mavericks in the second round. Despite having the highest scorer in every single game of the series, the Spurs lost in seven.

Besides some fringe bench players, the Spurs ran it back for the 2006–07 season. They struggled out of the gate and rumors of trades began swirling. With Bowen, Horry, and Barry all over the age of thirty-five, pundits began advocating for the team to trade them to invest in the youth of the roster. The Spurs stood pat. They ended 58–24 (again) and second in the division. Despite some early struggles and a third seed in their conference, the Spurs trashed the playoff competition.

They beat the Nuggets 4–1. They beat the "7 seconds or less" Suns in six games, though it was a controversial series. In the waning moments of Game 4, Horry decked Steve Nash into the scorer's table (Nash sold it a little bit, but Horry absolutely fucking muscled him). Things got heated afterward and Amar'e Stoudemire along with Boris Diaw (important players for the Suns who were on the bench at the time of the "decking") stepped onto the court to assist Nash. The rule at the time (which is still technically the rule now but it's… not as enforced I guess?) is that players could not leave the bench area. The two players were suspended for Game 5, crushing the Suns' roster. Nash told reporters after the game:

"That would be terrible if that silly play at the end of a game, when the game is really over, if that causes a detriment to the rest of the series."[75]

As Nash predicted, the Spurs won Game 5 with those two players gone and closed out the series in Game 6 when they returned. That was the hardest series they had that year.

---

75 Marc Stein, "NBA Suspends Stoudemire, Diaw for Leaving Bench," *ESPN*, May 15, 2007.

They beat Utah in five games and swept the Cavaliers in the Finals. Tony Parker became the first European-born player to win Finals MVP. Duncan was First Team All-NBA and All-Defense while Bruce Bowen joined him on the First Team All-Defense.

That was their third championship in five years (we covered four counting 1999), which solidified their dynasty.

FINAL THOUGHTS

What can we say about this dynasty? It is true that it's rare to add the number one overall pick to an already contending roster, but it's not impossible. In fact, two of the greatest examples of this situation have resulted in failure. The Detroit Pistons had the number two overall pick in the 2003 draft the year after making it to the Eastern Conference Finals. They took Darko Milicic (over Carmelo Anthony!) and while they would go on to win the championship that season, Darko was a massive bust. Had they hit on that pick, it is hard to think they wouldn't have been a dynasty.

Similarly, the Philadelphia 76ers traded for the number one overall pick in the 2017 draft. They selected Markelle Fultz, who dealt with many injuries and was traded to the Orlando Magic. While the jury is still out on Fultz (he actually had a low-key stellar first season in Orlando), the 76ers wasted that pick. Again, it is hard to picture the 76ers not being champions already had they added Jayson Tatum (third overall pick to Boston) to a core of Ben Simmons and Joel Embiid. So, yeah, the Spurs got lucky with the pick, but they still made the right choice. They also drafted two Hall of Famers with less glamorous draft picks: Parker at twenty-eighth overall and Ginobili in the second round.

Looking at the formula, we'll be taking the average from their title in 2003 up until their title in 2007. I could have covered it from their 1999 title, but much of the team's makeup changed between the titles, so I felt it wasn't part of the dynasty run. For five seasons, the Spurs had an average DS of 18.575. Their best season was the 2003 title, where Tim Duncan won MVP and Pop won COY.

What made a huge difference for the Spurs was their abundance of excellent role players. The Spurs had one of the best overall stars in the league. Duncan could score, defend, pass, all of it. Rather than surround him with more all-around players, the Spurs went out and got specialists. Bruce Bowen (defense), Brent Barry (shooting), and Manu Ginobili (all kinds of offense) were specialists in certain areas but excelled in those areas. The Spurs were one of two teams (the other being the Bulls) that we examined who had three +2 BPM role players in a season, and they did it three times (the Bulls did it twice).

The Spurs also made sure to bring in some guys with Dynasty DNA: Steve Kerr (Bulls) and Robert Horry (Lakers) were key contributors for several title runs. They were able to show up in the big moments, especially Horry. The Spurs, much like the Bulls and Lakers, were ready to replace key members of the lineup whenever needed. A big difference with the Spurs was their team culture. Guys like Duncan and Ginobili took pay cuts so the team could continue finding and paying surrounding talent. That is the difference between a couple championships and twenty-two straight playoff appearances.

EPILOGUE

I could easily cover the full twenty-two years (each one is impressive), but this is where the Spurs' dynasty comes to an end. Here are some quick hitters that cover the years after that 2007 title:

- Popovich was Coach of the Year again for both the 2011–12 season and the 2013–14 season (he is still the head coach and is still great)
- R.C. Buford won the Executive of the Year award twice in 2013–14 and in 2015–16 (he is still with the organization)
- Bruce Bowen retired after the 2008–09 season
- The Spurs met the Miami Heat in the 2013 Finals and lost
- The Spurs had a rematch with the Heat in the 2014 Finals and beat them (Kawhi Leonard was the Finals MVP)
- Tim Duncan retired in 2016; he is now an assistant coach under Popovich
- Manu Ginobili retired in 2018

CHAPTER 7:

THE GOLDEN STATE DYNASTY

———

After the 2018–19 season ended, the Warriors had just completed one of the most dominant runs in league history. Through brilliant drafting, shrewd free agency signings, and timely trades, the Golden State Warriors have won three of the last five titles, and they have been in the Finals for every year of that run. Before this success, however, they were the model of a poorly run organization. Here are some quick hitters on the team:

- Philadelphia Warriors from 1946 to 1962
- San Francisco Warriors from 1962 to 1971
- Golden State Warriors from 1971 to present
- Only title before this run was in 1975
- Missed the playoffs from 1994 to 2006
- Only one playoff series win from 1991 to 2012

When they first made the playoffs with Stephen Curry and other parts of their eventual championship core, it was in

2013. It would be the first time they made the playoffs since 2007 and only the second time since 1994. Before that, they had not made the Conference Finals since 1976.

The Warriors were one of those teams that was always in between playoff contention and the cellar. Some years they would be good enough to sneak into the playoffs; some years they would be bad enough to sneak into the top ten of the draft. But most years they were just good enough to barely miss the playoffs and be left with a lottery pick that may as well have been a regular one.

The fans had some fun teams along the way, with the We Believe team of 2007 being the most recent. They had very little substantial success, however. So how did the Warriors go from almost never making the playoffs to rattling off five straight Finals appearances? It all started in 2009.

THE FIRST BUILDING BLOCK

It was the day of the 2009 NBA Draft. The lottery balls gave the Warriors the seventh pick. The Warriors' general manager at the time, Larry Riley, was in deep negotiations with then-Suns' general manager, Steve Kerr (yeah, he's around) to trade their pick for Amar'e Stoudemire. The three most likely picks in that range were all point guards, and the Warriors already had a dynamic scoring guard in Monta Ellis. Flipping that pick for a high-grade veteran big man seemed like the logical move.

However, the second that Minnesota left Stephen Curry on the table after their number five and number six picks (sorry Wolves fans), there were no negotiations to be had. The Warriors had Curry as their number two in the draft and were never going to trade the pick if he fell to them. Larry Riley, in a Q&A with NBA.com recalled the reaction when Curry fell to them:

"There weren't a lot of high fives or anything like that, but everybody's looking at each other with a gleam in their eye, saying, 'OK, we're in good shape here.'"[76]

Curry made an impact right away. He averaged 17.5 points, 5.9 assists, 4.5 rebounds, and nearly two steals a game. He did all of this while shooting a blistering 43.7 percent from three. He was the Western Conference Rookie of the Month for three months and was named All-Rookie First Team. While he would finish second to Tyreke Evans in the Rookie of the Year race, it was clear the Warriors had something in Curry.

The Warriors finished thirteenth in the West. The team was bought by Joe Lacob and others in July 2010. As a part of "ushering in a new era," Lacob fired longtime coach, Don Nelson, and promoted assistant Keith Smart to head coach.

The 2010–11 season did not treat the Warriors well. Acquiring David Lee in a sign-and-trade in the off-season would be the only positive. Their number six overall pick, Ekpe Udoh, busted badly. He would never average more than five points

---

76   Scott Howard-Cooper, "On the Clock: Q&A with Former Golden State Warriors GM Larry Riley," *NBA*, June 8, 2017.

a game in a season. It did not help that Paul George and Gordon Hayward went just a few picks later (both All-NBA caliber players).

Curry picked up right where he left off the season before, but he twisted his right ankle several times over the course of the season. While he missed just eight games, he would undergo surgery in the off-season to repair and strengthen some torn ligaments in the ankle. That right ankle would become a looming shadow over Curry and the Warriors alike in the coming seasons. The Warriors finished twelfth in the West. Smart was fired after his first year as head coach.

UNDER NEW MANAGEMENT

The 2011–12 season brought a lot of change for the organization. The new ownership group brought in Bob Meyers to be the eventual replacement for Larry Riley. They also hired "dynasty-guru" Jerry West (yeah, he's still around too) as a top executive and consultant. They made Mark Jackson their first coach of the "new era." Jackson promised a defense-first approach and that his team would play hard regardless of the circumstances.

In the draft, the Warriors took Klay Thompson at number eleven. He would appear in every game of the lockout-shortened season for the Warriors and be named to the All-Rookie first team. Golden State had hit on another pick.

That would be the only good part of the team's season, however, as they would finish in the bottom three of the conference again. To make matters worse, Steph Curry missed forty games after injuring his right ankle multiple times throughout the season. He again had off-season surgery to address the issue. However, his injuries did play an important role in trade talks toward the end of the season.

It is rumored that the Milwaukee Bucks had a choice between Ekpe Udoh and one of Monta Ellis or Steph Curry in exchange for Andrew Bogut. Apparently, Curry's ankle injuries scared them off and they chose Ellis (sigh). Bogut was a former number one overall pick and had been third team All-NBA two seasons prior.

This was another important step in building the Warriors' dynasty. With Ellis gone, the Warriors signed Curry to a cheap four-year extension, as the fear over his injuries spread to his paycheck.

THE PLAYOFF RUN BEGINS

The 2012–13 season was the Warriors' best in a long time. The Warriors hit on not one, but two of their draft picks before the season. They owed a first-rounder that was top seven protected to the Utah Jazz, but they were determined to keep it. They even tanked the last game of the previous season to give them better odds (I'm not a huge fan of the whole "tanking" thing, but this is more strategic than anything else).

The basketball gods rewarded them as the lottery balls gave them exactly the seventh pick, allowing them to keep it. They took Harrison Barnes, a two-way wing out of UNC. In addition, they took Draymond Green at number thirty-five. Barnes was named First Team All-Rookie. While Green didn't make a considerable impression at the start, he would become an irreplaceable member of the Warriors' title team. The draft success was not the only measure on the season; they were hitting on all cylinders.

They made the playoffs for the first time since 2007. While Steph twisted his ankle on several occasions over the season, he missed just eight games. He also began to separate himself as the best shooter in the league, breaking the single season record for threes made (272, which is now ninth overall. It's a new age in basketball, people). David Lee became the first All-Star for the Warriors since 1994 and was also named to the All-NBA Third Team. Klay Thompson began to separate himself as a dangerous shooter as well, making 211 of his own threes.

Steph and Klay, a.k.a. the "Splash Brothers" as they became to be known, broke the single season record for threes made by two teammates (483). The Warriors earned the sixth seed and faced the fourth seed Denver Nuggets. Despite Andrew Bogut being the only member of the starting lineup with playoff experience, the Warriors beat the Nuggets in six games. They lost to the San Antonio Spurs in the next round, however. Despite the loss, the future looked very bright for the Warriors.

After their playoff run was stopped short, Bob Meyers went out looking for support for the 2013–14 season. They would add the last big piece of their first championship team in Andre Iguodala. The Warriors traded two first-round picks and two second-round picks to clear up the cap space to sign him—a high price that ended up bringing a great return.

Iguodala, funnily enough, was on the Nuggets team that had been eliminated by the Warriors a season prior. He received some backlash for joining the team that had beaten him. George Karl, the head coach for the Denver Nuggets then, even went as far as to say Iguodala was a "mole" for the Warriors in the playoffs the season before.[77] Iggy wouldn't be the only one to receive backlash for signing with the Warriors (foreshadowing alert!). The team, now with a savvy veteran star on the roster, began to flash signs of brilliance. They finished 51–31, only the fourth time in franchise history that they had won fifty or more games. This came despite injuries that forced several bench players and Iguodala to miss significant time.

One day before clinching the playoffs, Andrew Bogut suffered a broken rib that would keep him out of the playoffs. A successful season was cut short by that injury as the Warriors would fall to the Los Angeles Clippers in the first round. It was clear, though, that Curry was a star in this league now. He had made his first All-Star game and was named to the All-NBA second team. Early in the off-season, owner Joe Lacob and General Manager Bob Meyers were nearing an agreement to trade Klay Thompson to the Minnesota Timberwolves in return for star power forward Kevin Love. Reportedly, they both wanted it to happen. What changed their minds? Jerry West threatened to resign if they went

---

77 Ben Golliver, "George Karl Rips Mark Jackson's 'bush' Tactics, Identifies Andre Iguodala as 'mole,'" *Sports Illustrated*, November 29, 2013.

ahead with the deal. He was adamant that Thompson was a better fit for the team. He was right.

THE KERR REVOLUTION

The off-season before the 2014–15 season began with a shocker. Mark Jackson, the coach who turned around the franchise, was fired. This came even after a unanimous decision by the players to support him, but it didn't matter. Once more details emerged, it seemed like the firing of one of the most successful coaches in franchise history had been a long time coming.[78]

Two incidents in the 2013–14 season involving assistant coaches foreshadowed trouble. Brian Scalabrine was reassigned to coach in the D-League (now G-League) due to "disagreements" with Jackson. Another assistant coach was fired for secretly recording meetings with players and coaches. There was a report that Jackson had banned Warriors consultant, Jerry West, from practice, fearing that West's Hall of Fame resume would undermine him. One of his most heinous offenses involved backup center Festus Ezeli. When he went down with injury, Jackson told the team that Ezeli was rooting for them to fail, so that he would look like a better player. This lie culminated in the team confronting him and Ezeli breaking down mentally. Mark Jackson had turned the franchise around. It was time for him to turn it over.[79]

---

78 Tyler Conway, "Mark Jackson Fired by Warriors: Latest Details, Comments and Reaction," *Bleacher Report*, May 6, 2014.

79 Ibid.

The Warriors hired Steve Kerr as his successor. Kerr, as you already know, was a key member of the Bulls dynasty and had been an analyst for TNT in recent years. You may also recognize him from the beginning of this chapter, when he tried to trade for the pick that would eventually become Steph Curry. Ah, the circle of life. Kerr and the Warriors seemed like a match made in heaven, as Kerr knew what it took to win and set the career record for three-point percentage in his playing days. With him at the helm, the Warriors took off running. Kerr and Curry immediately grew a strong friendship, and Kerr knew how to coach him perfectly:

"Obviously [Curry is] so skilled and talented that you give him a lot of rope. Every once in a while, you have to reel him in if... you think that he's trying to do too much or missing something strategically that we're trying to do. You just tell him. He's easy to talk to. I'm really, really lucky to coach a star player who's so willing to accept criticism and respond positively to critiquing."
—KERR IN A *SPORTS ILLUSTRATED* INTERVIEW AFTER LESS THAN A YEAR ON THE JOB WITH THE WARRIORS[80]

They went 67–15, the best record in franchise history up to that point. Curry made the All-Star team for the second time and Klay joined him. Draymond Green, who stole the starting power forward spot from David Lee during the season, was named to the All-Defense First Team. Curry was named to the All-NBA First Team for the first time. He was the best

---

80 Rob Mahoney, "Fine Tuning: Coaching Stephen Curry, Best Shooter in the Universe," *Sports Illustrated*, April 7, 2015.

player in the league that season, evidenced by being awarded the NBA MVP award. He was just the second Warrior to ever win that award. Bob Meyers, the man who put most of the puzzle together, was the NBA's Executive of the Year. With all the regular season success and accolades on their shoulders, the Warriors went to the playoffs.

They swept the New Orleans Pelicans in the first round—easy money. They defeated the Memphis Grizzlies in the second round, a gritty defensive series. Moving on to the Conference Finals, they dispatched the Houston Rockets in five games. The Warriors spent very little time in trouble during those three series. They had reached the NBA Finals for the first time since 1975.

Their opponent: LeBron James and the Cleveland Cavaliers. Despite the Cavaliers losing their third-best player (Kevin Love, remember him?) early in the playoffs and their second-best player (Kyrie Irving) after just one game in the Finals, they played the Warriors tougher than any other opponent that year. After falling behind 2–1 in the series, Kerr made a decision that would change the landscape of the NBA for years to come. He started Andre Iguodala in place of Andrew Bogut. Going from a 7', 265-pound behemoth to a 6'6", 215-pound career swingman would have seemed like suicide. It wasn't.

The lineup of Curry, Thompson, Barnes, Draymond, and Iggy, was faster and shot better than any lineup on the Cavs. They could also switch nearly every matchup defensively with no issue. The Cavaliers would not win another game that series. For his part in swinging the Finals, Iguodala was awarded the Finals MVP award. The Warriors had built a championship team.

73–9 PLUS THE KDECISION

If 2014–15 was the dream season for the Warriors, the next regular season was heaven. The Warriors rolled into the 2015–16 season with nearly no discernible changes to their roster. They traded David Lee, who had lost nearly all his playing time anyway, to the Boston Celtics to save some money. They terrorized the league regardless.

The Warriors won the first twenty-four games of the 2015–16 season. It was the best start by any major league sports team in American history, and the second longest win streak in the NBA's history.

They finished the season 73–9, beating the Bulls' record of 72–10 in the 1995-96 season, and became only the second team ever to win more than seventy games. They won these games on the back of their "death lineup" as was coined whenever Iguodala would replace the center in the lineup.[81] Kerr rolled out that lineup relentlessly, knowing the league had no idea how to stop it. This was a new level of dominance in the NBA, and the lineup spawned the "small ball" philosophy. Teams began to hoard fast wings that could play limited minutes at center in an attempt to build their own death lineups. The winning and accolades came hand in hand for the Warriors.

---

81 Lee Jenkins, "The Birth of the Warriors' Death Lineup," *Sports Illustrated*, June 7, 2016.

Steve Kerr was named the Coach of the Year. Curry (First), Draymond (Second), and Thompson (Third) made All-NBA rosters and the All-Star roster. Draymond made his second straight First Team All-Defense appearance and broke a Golden State record with nine triple-doubles in a season. Curry won his second straight MVP award, becoming the first in NBA history to win the award unanimously.

They rode into the playoffs white-hot once again *and* lost only two games combined in the first two rounds of the playoffs. In the Conference Finals, however, they met the best team they had played in the entirety of this run, the Oklahoma City Thunder. The Thunder boasted two All-NBA players of their own in Russell Westbrook and Kevin Durant.

KD had won the MVP award the year before Curry won his first. The Thunder too, were a team built primarily from the draft. Their talent proved to be nearly too much for the Warriors, who found themselves in a 1–3 deficit. Then came the collapse. A combination of Thompson (forty-one points in Game 6) and Curry (thirty-six points in Game 7) exploding and the Thunder playing conservatively resulted in the Warriors coming back and winning in seven games. This result would cripple the Thunder franchise.

The reigning champions met the reigning Eastern Conference champions once again: the Warriors versus the Cavaliers. This time, however, LeBron had his budding stars. The death lineup once again proved to be impossible for the Cavs to stop, and the Warriors built a 3–1 lead. However, they followed the Thunder's wake—an epic collapse.

LeBron James averaged a near triple double and scored forty-one points in both Game 5 and Game 6. Draymond Green was suspended for Game 5 (a result of several flagrant fouls throughout the playoffs) and Curry was ejected (after he threw his mouthguard at a ref) in Game 6.[83] LeBron's explosion matched with the Warriors implosion, which meant there would be a Game 7. Game 7 was the only one in the series determined by fewer than ten points. It went the Cavs' way.

The Warriors became the first (and so far, the only) team to give up a 3–1 lead in the NBA Finals.

RIGHT PLACE, RIGHT TIME, RIGHT EVERYTHING

Sometimes it's better to be lucky than to be good. In the summer before the 2016–17 season, the Warriors were perhaps the luckiest team in NBA history.

They signed Kevin Durant. The team that broke the NBA record for wins in a season added a top five player and easily the best available player that year. So many factors went right for this to happen. If the salary cap didn't have a massive jump due to the new TV deal, the Warriors wouldn't have had space to sign him.[84] If they had not signed Steph Curry to a cheap extension while he was plagued with injuries, they wouldn't have had the money to spend on him. Had Harrison Barnes accepted the four-year sixty-four-million-dollar extension the Warriors had offered him earlier in the 73–9 season, they would have had no cap space at all. Lastly, had they won instead of lost against the Cavs, Durant wouldn't have dared join them.

However, all those factors broke right for them, and because of it, the Warriors were able to cement their dynasty. The Warriors already had as much talent as any other team and a playing style that maximized that talent. They would be contenders for many years. However, the loss showed that they could be susceptible to generational talents, such as LeBron James. Considering the state of the Eastern Conference at the time (in 2016–17, three Western Conference teams had a better regular season record than the number one team in the East—congrats), they would likely see him every single year. At the same time, teams in the West were only getting better. Considering these factors, the Warriors added another generational talent to their roster, ensuring they would be heads and shoulders above the competition for the foreseeable future.

Durant was heavily criticized for this decision by the media and his peers alike:

"Kevin is a terrific player, he's a good kid. But just disappointed with the fact that he weakened another team and he's gonna kind of gravy train on a terrific Warriors team. Just disappointed from a competitive standpoint."
—CHARLES BARKLEY[82]

---

82   Kelly Evans, "Charles Barkley Doesn't Respect Kevin Durant's Decision," *The Undefeated*, July 6, 2016.

He was criticized not just for joining the team that beat him, but for joining the best team in the league. While it is true that no easy route to a ring exists in the NBA, many argued that Durant took the easiest route in NBA history. After the season, Jerry West (who felt like his job was done) moved on to consult for the Los Angeles Clippers.

DYNASTY

Predictably, the Warriors were the best team in the league for the 2017–18 season. Harrison Barnes was a perfect fit for the starting lineup, and he was replaced by a superhuman version of himself. This new "Hamptons Five" lineup was even better than the death lineup, which was already killing teams.

They easily won the championship; Durant obtained his first ring. They only lost one game in the entirety of the playoffs, LeBron's Cavs being the only team able to steal a win. Their talent was far beyond anyone else in the league, and they played like it. They won again the next season, sweeping LeBron and sending him to Los Angeles in the process.

Their unrivaled dominance inspired a "super team" era in the NBA.

The Oklahoma City Thunder paired Russell Westbrook with All-NBA forward Paul George. The Houston Rockets, boasting the latest NBA MVP in James Harden, traded for All-NBA point guard Chris Paul. The Rockets would prove to be the biggest threat to the Warriors' legacy. They pushed them to seven games in the Western Conference Finals before succumbing. With that, the Warriors had made the Finals in four straight seasons, winning three championships. They had dynasty status.

During this two-year run, the Warriors collected another hoard of accolades. Meyers once again won Executive of the Year. Draymond was named Defensive Player of the Year. The team members combined earned six All-NBA selections and eight All-Star appearances.

THE FALL

The 2018–19 season remained the same for the Warriors in terms of their play. They added Demarcus Cousins in the off-season, meaning that they now had an All Star at each starting position. Cousins received criticism similar to Durant's. It would end up not mattering, as Cousins missed a lot of time due to injury and played inconsistently when he was healthy. The Warriors pummeled their opponents in the regular season regardless.

What did change that season, was what happened off the court. The rumor mill surrounded the Warriors all season (as it does with all dynasties), as Kevin Durant would soon be a free agent. It caused a level of anxiety surrounding the team that had not been there since Mark Jackson was stirring things up. This anxiety would turn ugly several times throughout the season, climaxing with a verbal altercation between Draymond Green and Kevin Durant after a close loss. Reports say that Draymond called Durant a "bitch," and said, "you're leaving anyways, we don't need you." Despite this, the Warriors were able to pull it together in the playoffs.[83]

They finished first in the Western Conference. Uncharacteristically, they lost two games in the first round to the undermanned but insanely gritty Los Angeles Clippers (who had been built by old friend Jerry West). They lost Durant to a calf injury in the next round against their rivals, the Houston Rockets. Regardless, the Warriors eliminated them in six games. In what seemed like a backward playoff run, they swept the Trail Blazers in the Conference Finals.

A massive piece of any dynasty is the ability to stay healthy. Despite Durant missing a little time and Curry missing some playoff games during the 2016–17 championship run, the Warriors were able to trot out their starting lineup for most of their dominant run. Making the playoffs and Finals every year takes a physical toll though, and it would catch up with them in the midst of their fifth straight Finals run.

The Warriors opened the series against the Toronto Raptors without Kevin Durant. They lost that game. They were able to pull it together in Game 2 to tie up the series. However, Klay Thompson missed Game 3 with an injury. Missing two of their best players, the Warriors lost that game. Despite Klay's return in Game 4, the Warriors lost and fell to an all too familiar 1–3 deficit. Game 5 is where everything was supposed to change. Kevin Durant was back from his injury. He made his first three shots, looking to take the series back.

---

83   Chris Haynes, "Sources: Draymond Green Suspended After Calling Kevin Durant a 'bitch,'" *Yahoo! Sports*, November 13, 2018.

However, he would rupture his Achilles tendon early in the game. Despite the Warriors winning that game, they looked shell-shocked after Durant's devastating injury. The Warriors lost Game 6 and Klay Thompson tore his ACL late in the game. The Raptors won their first NBA title.

FINAL THOUGHTS

The Warriors have the highest average dynasty score out of the teams we examined (21.75). After KD came into the fold, the Warriors essentially had four All-Stars and four combined All-NBA/All-Defensive players. They were damn good. Kerr qualified as Dynasty DNA for the entirety of the run for his time with the Chicago Bulls. Their best year was the 73–9 season where Curry won the MVP and Kerr won the COY (DS = 24, second to 72–10 Bulls). The Warriors had the greatest collection of talent still in their primes from at least 2000 and onward. It would be easy to discount their success due to what is perceived as a "weak move" by Kevin Durant. But we cannot ignore the job that Meyers and West did.

The Warriors drafted the three best players of their first championship and did not have to sacrifice any of them to add a fourth. They signed the perfect seasoned veterans to compliment them. Iguodala and Bogut did the dirty work and relished in it. What's more is that management had the confidence to fire the most successful coach in franchise history for someone that had not coached before, but whose ideals about the game matched the team perfectly. Steve Kerr was the prototype of the player that Steph Curry revolutionized. Curry is likely still a fire-breather from three without

Kerr, but he doesn't bend the game to his will without Kerr's insights.

Lastly, the Warriors changed the way the game is played. Much like Red Auerbach and Phil Jackson, Kerr implemented a style of basketball that no one had done (to that degree) and dominated basketball because of it. The influence of "small ball" is everywhere now. The Clippers have stocked up on two-way wings so they can play them on anyone. The Houston Rockets are even *starting* a 6'7" small forward at center (and it really worked for a small sample size). The Golden State Dynasty broke records, pissed fans off, and evolved the game into what it is today.

THE END?

Kevin Durant went to the Brooklyn Nets in free agency. The Warriors acquired All-Star D'Angelo Russell in the off-season. Andre Iguodala was traded for nothing to save cap space. Despite a revamping of the roster, the Warriors dynasty seemed to be over. With Klay Thompson healing for the entire season and Steph Curry nursing a broken hand for a majority of the season, the Warriors had the worst record in the league during the 2019–20 season. They traded Russell at the trade deadline for a tasty first-round pick and a potentially (emphasis on potentially) salvageable bust in Andrew Wiggins. Is this the end of the Warriors' dynasty? Potentially. Steph, Klay, and Dray are all still in the later third of their primes. Kerr is still at the helm, and the team is still committed to competing. What they do have now is some trade fodder.

Wiggins isn't worth much on the trade market but he has a big contract (he signed a five-year $146.5 million contract in 2017) that can be used to match a star's salary (you can also always convince a down-trodden team that he still has a ton of potential).[87] The Warriors will very likely have a top three pick in this upcoming draft, a potentially tasty trade piece. The Warriors cannot get someone of Giannis' level with just Wiggins and picks (despite what the blog boys try to tell you) but there is a slew of lower grade stars they could go after (Myles Turner, John Collins, and Jrue Holiday are possibilities). If they decide to package one of Dray or Klay (they'd never trade Curry) to that offer, big stars suddenly become more attainable (Karl Anthony-Towns and Joel Embiid come to mind). While we don't know if this is the end of the Warriors' dynasty, it certainly is the end of that iteration of the team. Whether they come back stronger than ever or not, they will look different.

FOREWORD TO
PART 3:

BONUS FUN

These are the Bonus Fun chapters. These are chapters that I wanted to write of my own volition. They feature either all-time teams (despite not qualifying for Dynasty status), examples of great players on less great teams, or teams that did almost everything right and still could not figure out the Dynasty puzzle. They are not in chronological order. Deal with it.

CHAPTER 8:

BIRD'S CELTICS

———

All right, guys. I have three reasons for writing this chapter. The first is that the Bird-era Celtics won three titles in six years and made four straight Finals appearances. They're an All-Time team, dynasty or not. The second reason is in case Bill Simmons reads this book, I need to make sure I don't get straight up murdered. Third, I'll find any excuse to write more about Red Auerbach. Let's start with Red in the 1979 off-season.

PLANTING THE SEEDS

So, the Celtics, despite spending two seasons at the bottom of the NBA, had a very solid roster. Cedric Maxwell, the twelfth overall pick in 1977, was starting at small forward. Tiny Archibald (sick name, no arguments allowed) was traded to the Celtics a year prior and was a three-time All-Star at point guard. They traded for Chris Ford, a sniper at the shooting guard position, in the 1978 off-season. Starting at center was Dave Cowens, already a Boston legend. Drafted in 1970, here's a list of his accolades heading into the 1979–80 season:

- Eight-time All-Star
- Three-time All-NBA
- Three-time All-Defense
- One All-Star MVP
- One MVP
- Two titles

He was a future Hall of Famer, but he was also aging, in the twilight of his career. They signed Gerald Henderson from the CBA to be their backup point guard. The team had a very solid overall roster, with a couple of stars. To push into contender status, however, they needed a megastar. Turned out, they already had him; he just had not played yet. Red Auerbach took a risk in the 1978 draft and took Larry Bird. The reason it was a risk was because everyone knew that Bird was going to play out his senior year at Indiana State (at this time, teams could draft players still in college and hold their draft rights whenever they decided to jump to the NBA). Even though he could have gone down with an injury that season and regardless would not have been available, Auerbach took a shot on "The Great White Hope." While executives around the league criticized and questioned the move, Auerbach had said that Bird was always his guy:

"I knew he was a great shooter, but I didn't know how great. I knew he was a great passer and rebounder, but I didn't know how great. And I did not know he would play with injuries; Larry was the most self-motivated player I have ever seen."[84]

---

84 Chris Reichert, "The Original 'Draft and Stash' Player," *Fansided*, 2017.

So, Bird was ready to debut in the 1979–80 season. But not before some drama. Auerbach and the current owner of the Celtics had been feuding for over a season. This is actually a super wild story so I'm going to summarize it real quick:

- In 1978, the current Celtics owner, Irv Levin, swapped franchises with the current Buffalo Braves owner John Y. Brown Jr (I found old newspaper clippings from this time and they actually just say "they agreed to swap" so I guess that was just a thing they could do).
- In addition to the swap, the owners agreed to a six-player trade so the owners would have some of their favorite players on their new teams.
- Boston sent Freeman Williams, Kevin Kunnert, and Kermit Washington (remember when he almost murdered a guy a couple chapters back?) to the Braves in return for Tiny Archibald, Billy Knight, and Marvin Barnes.
- Auerbach and new owner, Brown, immediately got off on the wrong foot as Auerbach was not consulted on this trade.
- In the 1979 off-season, Brown traded two first-round picks for Bob McAdoo (a future Hall of Famer at twenty-seven years old) without consulting Red.
- Brown sold the team in the 1979 season to Harry Mangurian after public backlash.
- Auerbach traded McAdoo almost immediately after Brown sold the team.[85]

After a dramatic off-season, the Celtics were ready to play. It was apparent almost immediately that Bird was a future

---

85   Leonard Shapiro, "Red Auerbach," *The Washington Post*, May 10, 1981.

great. He was the Rookie of the Year and made First Team
All-NBA. Bill Fitch, their head coach, was named the Coach
of the Year. The Celtics went 61–21, the first in the division. Bird and Tiny were both All-Stars. They swept Houston in the first round but fell to the 76ers (led by Dr. J) in
five games.

DYNASTY MOVES

Dave Cowens retired after the 1979–80 season. Red had no
issues replacing him. He probably made the most lopsided
trade of all-time prior to the 1980 season. He traded the first
overall pick and the thirteenth overall pick in the 1980 draft
for Robert Parish and the third overall pick, with which
they took Kevin McHale. Red and the Celtics secured two
future Hall of Famers and a top three front court of all
time for two first-rounders. Not too shabby. Parish, Bird,
and Tiny were all All-Stars. Tiny was the All-Star MVP.
Kevin McHale was the second straight Celtic to be named
to the All-Rookie First Team. Bird and Tiny (a great title
for a buddy cop movie) were named to the First and Second
All-NBA teams.

The team went 62–20, improving by one game from the previous season. They steamrolled Chicago in the first round. They
met the 76ers in the second round, the team that bounced
them the year prior. The 76ers had also gone 62–20 that season but lost the tiebreaker for the number one seed. They
quickly built a 3–1 lead on the Celtics, beating them the same
way they did the season prior.

This is where "Larry Legend" begins.

He led both teams in points and rebounds in Game 5 and Game 6, where the Celtics won both by two points. In Game 7, Bird hit a bank shot from the left side with barely a minute left, giving the Celtics a one-point victory. It was the first of many clutch moments for Bird. The newly constructed front court played a big role in hindering Dr. J in that series. They met the Rockets (led by Moses Malone) in the Finals and beat them in six games. Cedric Maxwell was awarded the Finals MVP trophy which, in retrospect, could have easily gone to Bird.

STAGNATION

The Celtics drafted Danny Ainge in the second round of the 1981 draft. While he wouldn't do much in his first season, it would be another brilliant draft pick by Auerbach. The team went 63–19, again improving by one game. They beat the Bullets 4–1 and set up yet another matchup with the 76ers. The 76ers again built a 3–1 lead against them and the Celtics were again able to come back and force a Game 7. The Celtics were nearly twenty balled on their home court in the decisive game and lost 120–106. Bird was again First Team All-NBA and made his debut on the Second Team All-Defense. He was also the All-Star game MVP. Parish was All-NBA Second Team, and Tiny joined his two teammates in the All-Star game.

The 1982–83 season was the low point for this iteration of the Celtics. Chris Ford retired, but Ainge was able to easily supplant him in the starting lineup. The biggest issue was that Tiny Archibald, now thirty-four years old, had clearly lost a step. He missed about a fourth of the season and was at the tail end of his career. The team went 56–26 and were second in the division. They beat the Hawks 2–1 in the first round but were swept by the Milwaukee Bucks (led by DPOY Sidney Moncrief) in the second round.

Fun Facts!

(1) this was the first time in franchise history that the Celtics were swept out of the playoffs. (2) Dave Cowens actually came out of retirement to play for the Bucks that season but missed this series against his old team with injuries.

Larry Bird had identical accolades to the season before, minus the All-Star game MVP. Parish was an All-Star and McHale made his debut on the All-Defense Second Team. After the season, Bill Fitch resigned and was replaced by K.C. Jones. The team was sold to Don Gaston.

NEW OWNER, NEW COACH, NEW DIRECTION

With new ownership and a new coach, Auerbach decided to take the Celtics into a new direction. He waived Tiny Archibald; he would go on to sign with the Milwaukee Bucks for one more season before retiring. He then traded two second-rounders and Rick Robey (solid backup center) to the Phoenix Suns in return for Dennis Johnson, a first-round pick, and a third-round pick. Johnson, already a four time All-Star and a great defender, became the Celtics' new starting point guard. Gerald Henderson was promoted to the starting lineup as his backcourt mate.

The Celtics, under a new youth movement, returned to their winning ways. They went 62–20 and were back at the top of the division. They beat the Bullets in four games. They scrapped with the Knicks (led by Bernard King) for seven games before the Celtics blew them out in Game 7. They met Tiny Archibald and the Milwaukee Bucks in the Conference Finals, beating them in five games. They ran into the Los Angeles Lakers, the reigning champs, in the Finals.

The Lakers versus Celtics showdowns in the '80s were legendary (this particular series was dubbed the "Showdown of '84"). Bird versus Magic. K.C. Jones versus Pat Riley. Jerry West versus Red Auerbach. Legendary duels at every level of the organizations. At the time, though, the Celtics owned the Lakers. They were 7–0 against them historically in the Finals. This year was no different. The Lakers, a team whose two best players (Magic and Kareem) were probably better than the Celtics, just didn't have the experience. They had swept the 76ers in the Finals the year before; they had not been truly tested yet. The Celtics' experience and physicality won in the end. The Celtics beat them in seven games, increasing the record to 8–0.

Bird won his first MVP along with his first Finals MVP. Bird, Parish, and McHale were all All-Stars. Dennis Johnson was Second Team All-Defense, along with Bird. McHale won the second ever Sixth Man of the Year award. Red Auerbach resigned as GM after the season, although he was still pulling strings with his new position as team president.

The 1984–85 season was more of the same for Boston. That is to say, more dominance. They started the off-season by trading Gerald Henderson for a first-rounder. Danny Ainge would return to the starting lineup to replace him. The team went 63–19, improving by one game (nearly a tradition at this point). Larry Bird won his second straight MVP. Dennis Johnson made his Boston All-Star debut and again made the Second Team All-Defense. Kevin McHale became the first player in NBA history to repeat as the Sixth Man of the Year.

The Celtics took care of the Cavaliers in four games in the first round. They dispatched an early version of the "Bad Boys" Pistons in six games in the second round. Philadelphia was no contest in the Conference Finals, with the Celtics dropping just one game against them. A rematch with those Lakers was up next.

The Lakers were on a revenge mission. All they wanted was the rematch against the Celtics, and they got it. The Celtics put a beating on them in the first game, winning by more than thirty points. But the Lakers would rally behind Magic Johnson and Kareem Abdul-Jabbar, winning four of the next five to finally take one from the Celtics. While it was Magic and Kareem's (awarded the Finals MVP) team, it is fun to note that Bob McAdoo (remember?) provided valuable minutes off the bench for the Lakers in that championship series.

ONE LAST RUN

Auerbach had one more flash of brilliance during this iteration of the Celtics. He traded Cedric Maxwell and a first-
round pick for Bill Walton, one of the most transcendent
centers the game had ever seen and also one of the most
injury-plagued. At the time, Walton was a two-time All-Star,
a Finals MVP, a two-time champ, and a regular season MVP.
That's the pedigree. He also had missed three full seasons due
to foot injuries including two straight from 1980 to 1982. He
had never played more than sixty-seven games in a season.
Boston's team doctors did not pass him on his medical tests,
claiming that his foot injuries had done too much damage.
Auerbach didn't care, pushing the doctors aside and asking
Bill himself as Walton recalls:

*"I'm lying on the table there in the doctors examining room. Red
looks down at me, and he says, 'Walton, can you play?' And I
looked up at him with the sad, soft eyes of a young man who
just wanted one more chance. One more chance to be part of
something special, to be part of the team, to be with the guys
one more time. And I looked up at him, and I said, 'Red, I
think I can. I think I can, Red.'"*[86]

So, Bill Walton played, and he played well. Bill Walton played
eighty games that season coming off the bench for the Celtics,
the most of his career. He was named the 1985–86 Sixth Man
of the Year, a testament to his impact.

Henry Mckenna, "Bill Walton Tells the Story of How He Ended up with
the Celtics," *Boston.com*, March 28, 2016.

> **Fun Fact!**
> The Celtics are the only team in NBA history to have three straight 6MOY players, which I think is especially cool considering the Celtics/Auerbach are credited with creating or at least popularizing the "sixth man" as a thing in the NBA.

The Celtics went 67–15, their best mark of this run. Bird won his third straight MVP, becoming just the third player to do so (no player has done it since). McHale, Bird, and Parish were all All-Stars. McHale and Johnson made the First and Second Team All-Defense, respectively. They swept the Bulls in the first round, beat Atlanta in five games, and swept the Bucks in the Conference Finals. They met the Rockets in the Finals, who had knocked out the Lakers behind their formidable frontcourt duo of Ralph Sampson and Hakeem Olajuwon. The Celtics were able to skirt by them in six games, including a blow out in Game 6. Bird was named the Finals MVP and the Celtics were champions again.

TRAGEDY AND DECLINE

Everything went wrong for the Celtics in the 1986–87 season. Bill Walton was only able to play ten games before going down with injury for the final time in his career. The team drafted Len Bias at number two overall. He was an electric player and was supposed to usher in a new era of Celtics basketball while also being able to supplant Bird and McHale in the twilight of their careers. Picture what James Worthy was for the Showtime Lakers. It was not meant to be. Less than forty-eight hours after the 1987 draft, Len Bias overdosed on cocaine and died—a tragic loss that crushed the Celtics.[87] The team went 59–23, an aging and injured team.

They swept the Bulls in the first round but would not have an easy time the rest of the playoffs. The Bucks pushed them to seven games, and it took thirty-one points from Bird and nineteen rebounds from Parish in that Game 7 to escape. They were again pushed to seven by a maturing Pistons team and it would take thirty-seven points from Bird in Game 7 to win by three (Bird made several clutch plays in the waning minutes of the game). They met their ultimate rivals, the Lakers, in the 1987 Finals.

The Lakers were just younger and more talented at this point. The Celtics were able to steal Game 3 and Game 5 but ultimately fell in six games. Michael Cooper was the DPOY that year, Magic Johnson was the MVP, and Kareem pulled out one last great series. They were simply too much. Bird was First Team All-NBA, joined by Kevin McHale. McHale and Johnson were both First Team All-Defense. Bird, McHale, and Parish were all All-Stars. They never made it back to the Finals with Bird after this season.

FINAL THOUGHTS

Just for fun, I ran the formula for the Bird Celtics, just to see how they measure up. From that 1981 championship up to the 1987 Finals loss, the Celtics had an average DS of 18.64.

---

87 Cindy Boren, "Remembering Len Bias 30 Years After His Death: 'He was It.'," *The Washington Post*, June 19, 2016.

That would have been third behind the MJ Bulls and the Golden State Warriors. Their best score came in the 1984 season (23.75) although the 1986 season was not far behind (22.625). The Celtics had a three-year run of having the MVP and the 6MOY in the same season (1984–86). None of the teams we observed ever had three straight MVPs and only had the 6MOY once in their run (if at all).

These Celtics had many things in common with the Auerbach teams of the past, namely the continuous pursuit of talent. Every instance that the Celtics lost a contributing player, Auerbach used it as an opportunity to find someone even better to replace them, just like he did with the Bill Russell Celtics. They chose players no matter what was thought of them, even medically. Bill Walton being able to play eighty games and win the 6MOY in that point of his career was likely an anomaly and something that should not have happened, but it did. It never would have happened if Auerbach had heeded the advice from his doctors. Larry Bird and the Celtics dueled with the Lakers for a majority of the '80s. They won some battles and lost some others. They had a Hall of Fame frontcourt and are remembered to this day for that.

CHAPTER 9:

LEBRON'S LEGACY

Bill Russel's Celtics made an NBA record ten straight Finals appearances, winning eight of them. Besides that, no team has made more than five straight Finals appearances (the GSW dynasty). However, one player led two different teams to a total of eight straight Finals appearances, winning three of them in a five-year span. Because two titles were won with different teams, neither team qualified as a dynasty in the original chapters. But this is as impressive a feat as any, and you know I had to talk about this player eventually. This is LeBron's Legacy.

LONG STORY SHORT

I'm going to summarize LeBron's first stint in Cleveland, as it is a long and grueling process that is honestly painful to look at. The Cleveland Cavaliers took LeBron James first overall in the 2003 draft. He was considered a sure thing coming out of high school and "Cleveland's Savior" because of his upbringing in Akron, Ohio. LeBron legitimized his hype almost immediately, easily winning the Rookie of the Year award in the 2003–04 season. Unfortunately, Cleveland's front office proved to be incapable of surrounding him with supreme talent. Throughout the seven years he spent in Cleveland, the team only had two non-LeBron All-Star appearances: Zydrunas Ilgauskas (a name for the ages) in 2005 and Mo Williams in 2009. Meanwhile, LeBron would stack up the following accolades:

- 2003–04 Rookie of the Year
- Six All-Star Game selections
- Six All-NBA selections (two Second Team and four First Team)
- Two First Team All-Defense selections
- Two All-Star MVP Awards
- Two League MVP Awards

The Cavaliers made five playoff appearances and won eight playoff series in those seven years. They made the Finals just once, where they were swept by the San Antonio Spurs. They just couldn't get anyone even close to LeBron's caliber to join up, and when they were given opportunities in the draft, they blew them (they took Luke Jackson at number ten in an admittedly awful 2004 draft). So, in the 2010 off-season, LeBron announced his decision to "take his talents to South Beach."

THE DECISION

Now listen, I don't blame LeBron for leaving the Cavaliers. If you read the section above, I don't think you can either. Honestly, I'm not all that upset he created a superteam in

Miami; the big three they put together hadn't played together (not counting Olympics/All-Star games), so it wasn't like he was joining a team that was already a superpower. The way he announced it though... oof. He ran a televised special dubbed "The Decision" where he made a spectacle of his free agency. Apparently, not even the teams that were courting him were aware of his decision when it aired.

It was done in poor taste and came off as a slap to the face of Cavaliers fans and players. Cavs' owner Dan Gilbert penned a letter condemning LeBron's actions and declaring that the Cavaliers would win a title before he did (spoiler alert: they did not).[88] Cleveland fans uploaded videos of them burning LeBron's Cavaliers jersey (this is commonly discussed as the first time this happened, which may or may not be true but it is definitely the first time a lot of people saw this).[89] The league treated the Heat and LeBron as villains for the 2010–11 season.

THE MIAMI YEARS

So, how did the Miami Heat build this super team? They were already a solid playoff team, a past contender who had won the title in 2006 but hadn't made it out of the first round of the playoffs since. At the time they were led by Dwyane Wade, a six-time All-Star who was the Finals MVP on that 2006 title team. Pairing him with the two-time MVP in LeBron

---

88 Joseph Zucker, "LeBron James Says He Felt Dan Gilbert's Letter When He Left Cavs Was Racial," *Bleacher Report*, October 17, 2017.

89 Sopan Deb, "LeBron James Faces Backlash Unseen Since 'The Decision,'" *The New York Times*, October 15, 2019.

James alone would have made them a contender in the East. General Manager Pat Riley (remember him?) wasn't satisfied, however. They added Chris Bosh, a five time All-Star, in free agency as well.

The Heat had legitimate stars at shooting guard, small forward, and power forward. The starting lineup was rounded out with Mario Chalmers, a perfectly solid point guard, and a three-man center rotation of Udonis Haslem (Heat legend), Joel Anthony, and LeBron's old friend Zydrunas Ilgauskas (very happy I got to write this name again). Mike Miller and James Jones were veteran snipers off the bench.

The Heat went 58–24 and were first in their division. LeBron, Bosh, and Wade were named All-Stars. LeBron was selected to the All-NBA First Team and All-Defense Second Team. Wade was named to the All-NBA Second Team. The Heat sprinted through the Eastern Conference portion of the playoffs, dropping just one game apiece to the 76ers, Celtics, and Bulls. They met the Dirk Nowitzki-led Dallas Mavericks in the Finals, a tough defensive team made up of savvy veterans.

The Heat and Mavericks traded games and were tied 2–2, but the Mavs would take the last two games en route to their first title in franchise history. The difference maker was likely the rebounding margin: The Mavericks had three players with more rebounds than the Heat's leading rebounder (LeBron) in the series. LeBron was heavily criticized for his Finals performance, where he averaged less points than the other two stars on his team. The growing population of LeBron haters was only getting more confident.

The 2011–12 season was shortened to sixty-six games due to a lockout.[90] It was also one of LeBron James' best seasons. LeBron was on a mission to demolish the league. Honestly, I think he relished being the villain and receiving all the hate. It fueled him. He averaged twenty-seven points, nearly eight rebounds, and over six assists a game. He was First Team All-NBA and All-Defense. He won his third MVP award. Most importantly, he shut his critics up. The Heat went 46–20 and were again at the top of their division. The Knicks proved to be no challenge in the first round, as the Heat got them with the Gentlemen's Sweep (winning the first three games, "allowing" the other team to win Game 3, then closing it out in Game 4). They disposed of the Pacers in six games.

They met the Celtics in the Eastern Conference Finals. This was a team that had eliminated LeBron twice when he was in Cleveland. This was also their last season as a contender with their current core. The Heat won the first two games, the Celtics took the next two. They traded wins until a winner-takes-all Game 7 was all that remained. LeBron put up thirty-one points and twelve rebounds (both game highs) and the Heat won by double digits. The Celtics proved to be the toughest competitor that the Heat would see that postseason, as the Oklahoma City Thunder proved too young and were bested in five games in the Finals. LeBron was finally a champion and Finals MVP. While the haters would never go away (when do they ever?), they were definitely quieted after that season, and LeBron had his validation.

---

90 Howard Beck, "N.B.A. Reaches a Tentative Deal to Save the Season," *The New York Times*, November 26, 2011.

LeBron may have had validation but that didn't mean he was stopping there. In fact, 2012–13 was his best Heat season, averaging twenty-seven points, eight rebounds, and seven assists a game. He deservedly received his second straight and fourth overall MVP award (only four other players have accomplished this). He repeated his accolades from the season prior and was joined by his "Heatles" teammates as All-Stars for the third season in a row. Wade was All-NBA Third Team for the second straight season. The Heat also made a key acquisition before the season in Ray Allen. One of the best shooters of all time, Allen spent several seasons on the contending Celtics before deciding to join forces with LeBron and the Heat. This was a decision that still brings rage out of his former Celtic teammates (they didn't invite him to the team's reunion in 2017).[91] As it turned out, they would need him. The Heat went 66–15, first in their division.

They swept the Bucks in the first round ("Bucks in Six" started here, IYKYK) and lost just one game to the Chicago Bulls in the second round. They met a maturing Indiana Pacers team led by Paul George (who had just won the Most Improved Player of the Year award that season). The Pacers pushed them to seven games, but LeBron, who led all scorers in every single game of the series, scored thirty-two to advance to the team's third straight Finals appearance.

There they met the San Antonio Spurs, made up of an aging core of their previous dynasty in Tim Duncan, Manu Ginobili and Tony Parker paired with twenty-one-year-old rising

---

91 Scooby Axson, "Ray Allen Not Invited to '08 Celtics Championship Reunion," *Sports Illustrated*, March 20, 2017.

superstar Kawhi Leonard. The Spurs, led by Kawhi's super-glue defense on LeBron and Danny Green's superb shooting (set a record then for most threes made in a Finals series), had a 3–2 lead on the Heat. Game 6 was a shootout of epic proportions: ten ties and eight lead changes. The Spurs, looking to close out the series, led for nine more minutes than the Heat did.

San Antonio have a five-point lead with 28.2 seconds remaining. LeBron makes a three with 20.1 seconds remaining to make it 94–92. The Heat foul Kawhi Leonard. If he makes both free throws it becomes a two-possession game, basically sealing the deal as champions. He clanks the first, makes the second. 95–92. Three-point game. 19.4 seconds left. LeBron misses a three with 7.9 left on the clock, Bosh collects an offensive rebound and kicks it out. What happened next was one of the greatest shots in Finals history. Ray Allen hits a three with 5.2 seconds remaining. Tie fucking game. Spurs can't convert on the other end. The Heat go on to win in overtime and beat the Spurs in Game 7 for their second straight title. LeBron got his second straight Finals MVP award, only the second player in NBA history to win back-to-back MVPs and Finals MVPs (Jordan, of course, being the other one).

The team ran it back with little roster changes in the 2013–14 season. They went 54–28 and led their division once again, despite a lot of missed time from Wade. LeBron was All-NBA First Team and All-Defense Second Team. LeBron, DWade, and Bosh were all All-Stars. Once again, the East was no match for this team. They swept the Charlotte Bobcats (the one and only Bobcats reference in this book), dropped just one game to the Nets, and beat the always feisty Pacers in six games. They set themselves up with a rematch against the Spurs. Whether the team ran out of gas or were simply not as good as the Spurs, they just could not compete. They fell to the Spurs, losing all but one game. After the season, LeBron decided he had some unfinished business elsewhere in the NBA.

THE PRODIGAL SON RETURNS

LeBron went back to his roots, the Cleveland Cavaliers. He wanted to fulfill his promise of a ring to the state that raised him, and then was the best time to do it. Despite the scathing open letter written after he initially left the first time, Dan Gilbert welcomed LeBron back with open arms, as did the city of Cleveland. Let's do a quick summary of the four seasons that the Cavs had while Lebron was in Miami, or alternatively, how close they came to "winning a title before LeBron" (ha…).

- **2010–11:** 19–63. Cavs take Kyrie Irving at number one in the 2011 draft (good!) and Tristan Thompson at number four (Klay Thompson, Jimmy Butler, Kawhi Leonard still on the board).
- **2011–12:** 21–45. Kyrie wins Rookie of the Year. Tristan Thompson makes All-Rookie Second Team. Cavs take Dion Waiters at number four in the 2012 draft (Damian Lillard, Andre Drummond, Harrison Barnes still on the board) and Tyler Zeller at number seventeen (fine).
- **2012–13:** 24–58. Kyrie makes his first All-Star game. Dion Waiters makes All-Rookie First Team. Tyler Zeller makes All-Rookie Second Team. Cavs take Anthony Bennett at

number one overall in the 2013 draft (One of the biggest draft busts of all time. Victor Oladipo, Giannis Antetokounmpo, CJ McCollum still on the board).

- **2013–14:** 33–49. Kyrie makes his second All-Star game and is named the All-Star MVP. Cavs take Andrew Wiggins at number one overall. (He and Jabari Parker were the consensus 1A and 1B picks that year and have both disappointed in the NBA, so I'll cut the Cavs a little slack here).

So, in conclusion, one of the worst four-year stretches of an organization I have ever seen. They improved their win total over the course of the four seasons by fourteen games and were still nine games away from being .500. The team was continually given chance after chance in the draft (three number one picks!) and only came away with one player considered above average today. Yet, LeBron chose to give them another chance.

LeBron brought some old friends with him in Mike Miller and James Jones.

Fun Fact!

While the chapter is about LeBron going to eight straight Finals, James Jones was actually with him for every single one. The real Dynasty is the friends we made along the way.

The Cavs had LeBron and a star guard. Following the Miami blueprint, they wanted to pair them with a star power forward. So, they sent Anthony Bennett and Andrew Wiggins (the past two number one picks in the draft) and a first-rounder (that was rerouted to a third team) to the Minnesota Timberwolves in exchange for three-time All-Star Kevin Love.

The Cavs weren't done bringing in help, though. In January, with the team performing fine (but not spectacularly), they made a three-team trade for some more role players. At the end of the deal, they had sent out Dion Waiters, two end-of-bench guys, and a second-rounder in return for Iman Shumpert and J.R. Smith of the New York Knicks. I'll be real with you guys, as much as I've sarcastically berated the Cleveland front office in this chapter, this is a very, very solid trade. A borderline bust and a second-rounder for two legit role players and a first-rounder? I'll take that any day.

Then, of course, they turned around and traded that first along with another first for Timofey Mozgov. Mozgov was a solid if unspectacular player, who played Thompson's position not much better than Thompson himself. Mozgov was a perfectly fine player at the time, but two first-rounders? Yeesh. Anyway, it didn't matter because LeBron is LeBron and he laid waste to the Eastern Conference.

The team went 53–29. They swept Boston in the first round but lost their star forward Kevin Love due to a separated shoulder (it was never proved that Kelly Olynyk injured him on purpose, but it looked dirty as hell). He was out for the playoffs. This made the second round a bit more difficult, but they were still able to beat the Bulls in six games. They played the first overall seed in the sixty-win Atlanta Hawks and, of course, swept them.

They met up with the Golden State Warriors in the Finals. They lost Game 1 and, to make matters worse, they lost Kyrie Irving to a broken knee cap. Despite this, LeBron dropped thirty-nine points and sixteen rebounds in Game 2 and forty-four points in Game 3 to lead the series 2–1. LeBron's heroics and Matthew Dellavedova's surprisingly effective defense on Stephen Curry brought light to the Cavs' chances. But LeBron couldn't do it all. I mean, he did lead all players on either team in points scored, rebounds, and assists. So, he could do it all, just not win like that. The Warriors took the next three and sent LBJ packing.

The 2015–16 season didn't start well for the Cavaliers. Despite bringing in established veterans in Mo Williams and Richard Jefferson, the team was struggling out of the gate. This development, coupled with Kyrie missing thirty games of the season, spelled trouble for the Cavaliers. They fired their coach, David Blatt, after forty games and promoted assistant Tyronn Lue (of Lakers and AI fame). Lue allowed the team to play a little freer and fully put the offense in LeBron's hands. It worked. The team went 57–25 and earned the one seed in the Eastern Conference.

The team swept the Pistons and the Hawks in the first two rounds. The Raptors took them to six games in the Conference Finals, but it wasn't all that close. They earned a rematch with the Warriors, who had just gone 73–9, breaking the all-time record for wins in a season. The Cavaliers lost Games 1 and 2 by a combined forty-eight points. They won Game 3 by thirty points but dropped Game 4. Things looked grim; after all, no team had ever lost a 3–1 lead in the Finals before. The Cavs were able to pull off a win in Game

5 and, much to the chagrin of Warriors fans, Draymond Green was suspended for Game 6. (Listen man, you can be upset about that decision all you want. The guy spent most of playoffs dick-kicking opponents and throwing himself at players' legs. Zero sympathy from me.) With Green removed from the game, Cleveland took Game 6 on their home court.

They had tied up the series. Winner-takes-all Game 7, baby. Eleven ties and *twenty* lead changes. This was a game for the ages. With 4:39 left on the clock, Klay Thompson tied the game at 89. No one would score again until there was just fifty-three seconds left. With 1:50 on the clock, Andre Iguodala (who had won the Finals MVP last season) went up for a seemingly easy and death-sentencing layup. LeBron came out of nowhere and, well, as Mike Breen said:

"OH, BLOCKED BY JAMES!"[92]

That remains one of the most clutch defensive plays in Finals history and one of the best broadcasting moments in league history. Anyway, back to fifty-three seconds left on the clock. Kyrie Irving hits a three from twenty-five feet over Steph Curry. Another classic clutch moment. That was it. I know there was fifty-three seconds left on the clock. It didn't matter; the Warriors didn't score again. LBJ added a free throw in the waning seconds to make it a 93–89 final. They had become the first team in league history to overcome a 3–1

---

92 Dave McMenamin, "When LeBron Swooped in and Changed the Course of Cavs' History," *ESPN*, June 27, 2016.

lead in the Finals, conjuring up memes that would continue for years ahead.

LeBron won the Finals MVP award—in case you wondered why—by leading both teams in points, rebounds, assists, steals, and blocks. Not only had that never happened in a Finals series before, it was the first time in a playoff series. An all-time Finals appearance from The King, and he did it for his hometown:

"CLEVELAND, THIS IS FOR YOU!"[93]

ALL DOWNHILL FROM HERE

The 2016–17 season should have been a victory lap for the Cavaliers. Yes, they lost Dellavedova to the Milwaukee Bucks, but they traded for Kyle Korver to shore up their bench. Instead, the Warriors stole the show. Remember how I said they broke the record for wins the season prior? Well, they added the second-best player on the planet in Kevin Durant afterward. The best overall team in the league now had one of the two (Kawhi being the other) players that could go "mano y mano" against LeBron. The Cavs went 51–31, second in the East. They swept Indiana and Toronto and lost just one game against the Celtics. Didn't matter. Warriors beat them in five. They had created the ultimate unfair team; no one was touching them.

---

93 Zach Harper, "LeBron James After Winning the 2016 NBA Finals: 'Cleveland, this is for you!'" *CBS Sports*, June 19, 2016.

Before the 2017–18 season, Kyrie demanded a trade. The Cavaliers front office traded their superstar point guard for Jae Crowder (a solid 3 and D guy), Ante Zizic (a prospect at center), a good first-rounder, two second-rounders, and Isiah Thomas. Isaiah Thomas had been an All-NBA guy the season before. That season had been cut short by a gnarly hip injury that many said to stay away from. The Cavaliers didn't listen, and Isiah Thomas never got close to his All-Star season again. They signed former MVP Derrick Rose (who was one season away from deciding he wasn't washed anymore) and an aging friend in Dwyane Wade. The team under-performed and at the trade deadline, they let all hell break loose:

- In a three-team trade, the Cavs sent out Jae Crowder, Derrick Rose, Iman Shumpert, and two second-rounders in return for George Hill and Rodney Hood of the Utah Jazz.
- They traded Isiah Thomas and Channing Frye to the Los Angeles Lakers in return for Jordan Clarkson and Larry Nance Jr.
- They Sent Dwyane Wade to the Miami Heat for a second-rounder (this was done as a favor to Wade, who would have seen all of his minutes lost with the newcomers).

Despite the chaos and carelessness of the Cleveland front office, the new core actually gelled better than the last one and the Cavs seemingly had one more run left in them. They struggled against a feisty young Pacers team led by Victor Oladipo but beat them in seven. They swept the Raptors who, by the end of the "LeBron: King of the East" era, basically rolled over every time they saw him in the playoffs (they were referred to as "LeBronto."[94] It was bad, guys). They were again tested by a young, well-coached Boston Celtics in the Conference Finals (this is actually the team that the Cavs traded Kyrie to, but he was out for the season with a knee injury during this series) but were able to again squeak by in seven.

The Cavs (I guess I can just say LeBron at this point) met the Warriors again and were swept. The following off-season, LBJ took his talents to Los Angeles, where the Lakers missed the playoffs in his first season—thus, ending the eight-year Finals run on which Lebron had embarked. LeBron is now paired with All-NBA forward Anthony Davis in Los Angeles and is seemingly on the cusp of bringing championships back to the Lakers.

FINAL THOUGHTS

Just for my own personal satisfaction, I ran the 2007 Cleveland team (that made the Finals) through the formula. They got a 9.375. That deserves at worst a humorous exhale from your nose. Unfortunately, it doesn't get much better. The eight-year straight Finals run had an average Dynasty Score of 15.76—which would have been dead last in our rankings. The Miami years are a little better, with an average of 18.81 over the four years. An average of 12.whocaresyouknowitslow in the four years after in Cleveland. That's a bit rough. The best year was 2013 (DS = 20.375). LeBron won the MVP and the Heat had five contributing role players. The biggest issues

---

94 Kyle Newport, "Mark Jones Calls Toronto 'LeBronto' as LeBron James Lights up Raptors in Game 2," *Bleacher Report*, May 3, 2018.

with these teams were the support and the defense. The Heat never once had a role player with a +2 BPM. The Cavs had just one (two when Kevin Love didn't make the All-Star team). The Miami teams only ever had one player on the All-Defense teams—LBJ. The Cavs didn't have any. This chapter is a lesson in how far generational talent gets you, but how limited it can be without proper support.

CHAPTER 10:

THE DYNASTY THAT NEVER WAS

———

I opened this book with a story about the Brooklyn Nets: a big city team that made wrong decision after wrong decision in an attempt to "buy" a dynasty. The subject of this chapter is kind of like that. It is also very different.

The Oklahoma City Thunder did so much right. With the talent they cultivated through the draft, it was almost impossible for it not to lead to championships. Sometimes though, it just isn't meant to be. See what I mean below.

THE BEGINNING

In 2009, the Oklahoma City Thunder assembled one of the best drafted teams (arguably) of all time. Sam Presti started this three-year run of stellar drafting by selecting Kevin Durant with the number two pick in the 2007 NBA draft. Durant was a sure thing in the league, and would go on to win Rookie of the Year that season. The team, then the Seattle Supersonics, moved to Oklahoma City after Durant's first season. The next year, Presti took Russell Westbrook at number four and Serge Ibaka at number twenty-four in the 2008 draft. Westbrook made the All-Rookie first team while Ibaka stayed overseas for another year. The Thunder had selected two franchise stars in back-to-back drafts. Presti wasn't done. He selected James Harden at number three in the 2009 draft. Harden made the All-Rookie second team that season. If you were to ask experts at the time whose future they would take for the next five years, every single person would have said the Thunder.

THUNDER RISING

In the three years during those drafts, the Thunder did not finish higher than thirteenth in the Western Conference. The year they drafted Harden, however, things began to change. The Thunder made the playoffs for the first time in Oklahoma City. While they were just an eight seed, they pushed the number one seed Lakers (who would go on to win the title that season) to six games. With wins on the rise, accolades soon came as well. Kevin Durant made the All-Star game, was the NBA scoring leader, and made first team All-NBA for the first time. He was a rising superstar. At the same time, James Harden made the all-rookie second team, and OKC Coach Scott Brooks won Coach of the Year. After the season, the Thunder inked Durant to a five-year extension. There was no question about where their franchise player would be for the near future. Their ascent did not stop there.

The 2010–11 season would see Russell Westbrook join Durant in the ranks of NBA elite. He made the All-Star game and made an All-NBA (second) team for the first time. Durant secured his second straight scoring title, and again made First Team All-NBA. OKC now had budding stars on their roster. Westbrook's breakout led to more winning. The Thunder finished fourth in the West that season. They won their first playoff series in Oklahoma's history, beating the Nuggets in five games. They advanced to their first Conference Finals after beating the Grizzlies in seven games. Their playoff run would end at the hands of the Mavericks, who beat them in five games. The Mavericks would go on to win the title that season. The Thunder were improving every year and their championship-caliber squad was on the cusp of a dynasty.

THE PEAK

The 2011–12 season was the peak for this iteration of the Thunder. Every player we mentioned before made their mark on the league. Let's summarize:

- Kevin Durant: All-Star Game MVP, First Team All-NBA, Third Straight Scoring Record (first player since MJ)
- Russell Westbrook: All-Star and Second Team All-NBA
- James Harden: Sixth Man of the Year
- Serge Ibaka: First Team All-Defense, led league in blocks per game

The Thunder had more accolades than any other NBA team at the time.

This was the team's peak in playoff success as well. They ended the regular season as the number two seed in the West. They exacted revenge on the Mavericks, sweeping them in the first round. The Thunder got some more revenge in the second round, beating the Lakers in five games. The Thunder secured their first Finals berth in Oklahoma history. However, they would lose to the Miami Heat in five games.

THE BEGINNING OF THE END

In the off-season after losing in the NBA Finals, the Oklahoma City Thunder traded James Harden to the Houston Rockets for Jeremy Lamb, Kevin Martin, and two first-round draft picks. OKC and Harden couldn't agree on a contract extension that suited the Thunder's desire to remain under the luxury tax.[95] Harden was a rising player but the return OKC got for him was more than fair… for who he was at the time. Houston signed Harden to a big extension the second he touched down in the city; they were betting he wasn't finished developing. They were right. Harden would debut in his first All-Star game that season and make his first All-NBA team (third team).

Despite the loss of Harden, the accolades continued to pile up for OKC. Durant was again first team All-NBA and Westbrook was again third second team All-NBA. Ibaka paced the league in blocks per game and made the first team All-Defensive roster for the second straight year.

---

95 Golliver, Ben, "Grade the Trade: Thunder Trade James Harden to Rockets," *Sports Illustrated*, October 28, 2012.

The Thunder kept winning games as well. They finished atop of the Western Conference for the first time. They met the Houston Rockets, led by their former Sixth Man of the Year, in the first round. The Thunder took care of them in six games, making everyone in Oklahoma feel a little bit better about that trade. They lost embarrassingly in five games to the Grizzlies. This was their worst playoff run since first making the playoffs with Durant and Westbrook. Reports of Durant's unhappiness began to circulate.[96]

MVP SEASON PLUS THE LOST SEASON

The 2013–14 season was a special year for OKC fans. Kevin Durant finally won an NBA MVP award. After securing his fourth scoring title in five years, starting in his fifth straight All-Star game, and making his fifth straight first team All-NBA, he was a shoo-in. The Thunder had the best player in the league. However, their other star was ailing. Westbrook had had surgery on his knee before this season. He missed a big chunk of the year and subsequently did not qualify for any accolades. Nevertheless, Durant put the team on his back. The Thunder still finished second in the West and dominated the playoffs. Avenging the previous season's loss to the Grizzlies, the Thunder won in seven. They then beat the Clippers in six. They fell once again in the Conference Finals to the Spurs. (Guess what the Spurs were? The eventual champions. A bit of a theme here, no?)

96   Spears, Marc J., "The KD Question: Did Kevin Durant Play His Last Game for the Thunder?" *The Undefeated*, May 31, 2016.

The following 2014–15 season was the lost season. Durant missed the first seventeen games of the season. He would only play in twenty-seven games total. The Thunder missed the playoffs for the first time since they started this run. Westbrook was named the All-Star MVP and made second team All-NBA. James Harden made his second straight first team All-NBA roster for the Houston Rockets. The Thunder's longtime coach, Scott Brooks, was fired a week after the season concluded. Tensions began to build.

LEGEND OF THE 3–1 LEAD

This was the year. Kevin Durant was a free agent after the 2015–16 season. The Thunder had to convince him to stay. New coach, Billy Donovan, had to make a connection with him. The Thunder finished third in the conference. They easily beat the Mavericks in five games in the first round. They ran past the Spurs in six games (retiring Tim Duncan in the process). Next, they met the hardest team they had played in their careers: the 73-9 Golden State Warriors, which consisted of MVP Steph Curry, first team All-Defense Draymond Green, and All-NBA Klay Thompson. They made up perhaps the only other team in history that arguably could be called "Best Drafted Team." The Thunder built a 3–1 lead against the Goliath. Then came the collapse. They became only the tenth team in NBA history to blow a 3–1 lead in the playoffs. The ramifications of this comeback affect the league even today. The Warriors would go on to the Finals… and become themselves the first team in league history to blow a 3–1 lead in the Finals.

AN UNMERCIFUL END

The playoffs may have ended, but the competition was far from over in Oklahoma. An all-out pursuit of Kevin Durant began. Big market teams and top-tier basketball organizations began making their pitches. The Boston Celtics, hometown Washington Wizards, and San Antonio Spurs were in the thick of things. The Golden State Warriors were rumored to be involved, but at the time no one thought Durant would dare join the best team in the league. If the Thunder were going to go down, however, they were going to go down fighting.

Sam Presti sent Serge Ibaka to the Orlando Magic for Victor Oladipo, Ersan Ilyasova, and Domantas Sabonis. He had turned one of the "core four" into three rotation players, two of which could have star power. Considering Ibaka was on an expiring contract, this was an incredible move. Ultimately, it wouldn't matter. On July 4, 2016, Kevin Durant announced that he was leaving the Oklahoma City Thunder to join the 73–9 Golden State Warriors. One of the top three talents in basketball decided to join the team that had broken the record for wins in a season. This hurt OKC fans and basketball fans alike. The Thunder lost their franchise player for nothing. Ibaka was gone as well; only Westbrook remained.

LIFE WITHOUT KD

Westbrook was on a mission in the 2016–17 season. Determined to overcome the loss of Kevin Durant, Russell took it out on his opponents. He became only the second player in

NBA history to average a triple double over a full season. He finished first team All-NBA. He became the second Oklahoma City Thunder player to win the Regular Season MVP award. The Thunder finished sixth in the West and lost in five games to James Harden and the Houston Rockets. The Golden State Warriors won the NBA Championship and Kevin Durant won the Finals MVP award. Westbrook signed a five-year Supermax extension after this season, making sure he was the one who "stayed."

LONG REST-OF-STORY SHORT

- After the 2016–17 season, Sam Presti traded Victor Oladipo and Domantas Sabonis for Paul George. He traded what he got for Serge Ibaka to get Westbrook a second superstar. Masterful.
- Westbrook followed up his historic season by being the first player to average a triple double for two straight seasons, and he made it three straight the following season.
- The Thunder would lose in the first round the next two years, making it three straight first-round exits after Durant's departure.
- James Harden won the MVP award with Houston in the 2017–18 season.
- After the 2018–19 season, Sam Presti traded Paul George to the Los Angeles Clippers for the biggest haul ever in a trade for a superstar.
- A few weeks after the PG trade, Presti traded Russell "Mr. OKC" Westbrook to the Houston Rockets. This

concluded the "Core Four" story once and for all. West-brook reunited with his old teammate, James Harden, in Houston.

- Kevin Durant won two titles in GS, winning Finals MVP both times. He joined the Brooklyn Nets via free agency after the 2018–19 season. He is currently recovering from an Achilles Tendon rupture.
- Serge Ibaka won a title with the Toronto Raptors during the 2018–19 season, becoming only the second "Core Four" player to win a title. He came off the bench.

FINAL THOUGHTS

That's it. The Thunder drafted three MVPs in three years and have basically nothing to show for it. It isn't even like they botched every possible thing like a certain Midwestern team did with LeBron. No, Sam Presti surrounded his star player with as much star power as possible. But it wasn't enough. Maybe it was the coaching; neither Scott Brooks or Billy Donovan ever really figured out how to mesh Durant's and Westbrook's playing styles seamlessly. Maybe it was the role players. While it was true that the Thunder had four very good players, they were often surrounded by very mediocre role players. Having stars simply isn't enough. Let's contrast this situation with the Warriors, who basically stole the Thunder's dynasty.

The Thunder had an MVP caliber player at Point Guard, Shooting Guard, and Small Forward. Ibaka served as a strong two-way option. The Warriors had an MVP caliber player at Point Guard and Stars at Shooting Guard and Power Forward. The Thunder won in that capacity. The difference is that the Warriors had very solid options starting at small forward and center, with at least three strong reserves coming off the bench. The Thunder did not have that, to say the least. The biggest difference is likely Steve Kerr. Kerr may not be twice the coach that Scott Brooks is (although I'm not convinced) but he was the perfect coach for that Warriors team. He took his players to heights they had only dreamed of because his system suited them perfectly. It's those other factors that take you from tasting success once to dining on it nightly.

The Thunder had all the makings of a potential dynasty. They could have ruled the NBA for a decade. For one reason or another, none of that happened.

BONUS FACTS

- The Thunder made the playoffs six times with Kevin Durant. Four times out of six, the team the Thunder lost to in the playoffs went on to win the NBA title. Only one of the six teams failed to make the Finals.
- At least one of Durant, Harden, and Westbrook has been first team All-NBA each season for the past ten years.
- Durant, Harden, and Westbrook won three MVPs in a six-year span.
- Sam Presti did not win Executive of the Year in any of the seasons following these historic drafts.
- Harden, Durant, and Westbrook have broken and currently hold forty-two NBA records combined.

CONCLUSION

___

The conclusion of this book was mainly contingent on the conclusion of the NBA season. It is the year 2020. While the champion would not have been decided yet, the Finals would have begun by my June 5 deadline (best believe I'm cutting it close folks). However, the NBA season has been suspended since March. The COVID-19 pandemic has forced all sports leagues to pause for the time being.[97] The NBA has a plan to resume in late July and play out the rest of the season in some form.[98] I can still do the conclusion I wanted to do for this book, but it is going to take a little more critical thinking (sigh).

We're going to run all thirty NBA teams through the formula—all eight categories. The five teams with the highest Dynasty Scores will be given paragraphs on what made their scores so high, and how close they appear to being a dynasty. Unfortunately, we have no idea when or if the NBA will

97 Dan Woike, "NBA Suspends Season Indefinitely Over Coronavirus Pandemic," *Los Angeles Times*, March 11, 2020.
98 Marc Stein, "N.B.A. Owners Set a July 31 Restart, All in Florida," *The New York Times*, June 4, 2020.

announce the award winners and All-NBA/Defense rosters. So, we're coming up with our own.

I scoured article after article and held debates with several peers to come up with these lists. Every award will have two winners (no matter how big the gap is between one and two) just so we can cover all our bases. The points for said award will be attributed to both players and their respective teams. For the All-NBA teams, it is usually three teams of five. We're just going to do the top twenty players in the NBA this season, plus one extra team (to cover our bases, of course). The same will go for the All-Defense teams; the top fifteen defensive players (as opposed to the usual ten) get a nod. They will be listed randomly, with no "1st/2nd/3rd/whatever" designation. Because this is only for the purposes of the formula, awards like Executive of the Year and All-Rookie teams will not be forecast. The same goes for the All-Star teams, which were announced earlier this season. Away we go.

MOST VALUABLE PLAYER

- Giannis Antetokounmpo, Milwaukee Bucks
- LeBron James, Los Angeles Lakers

ROOKIE OF THE YEAR

- Ja Morant, Memphis Grizzlies
- Zion Williamson, New Orleans Pelicans

DEFENSIVE PLAYER OF THE YEAR

- Anthony Davis, Los Angeles Lakers
- Giannis Antetokounmpo, Milwaukee Bucks

SIXTH MAN OF THE YEAR

- Dennis Schroeder, Oklahoma City Thunder
- Montrezl Harrell, Los Angeles Clippers

MOST IMPROVED PLAYER

- Brandon Ingram, New Orleans Pelicans
- Bam Adebayo, Miami Heat

COACH OF THE YEAR

- Nick Nurse, Toronto Raptors
- Mike Budenholzer, Milwaukee Bucks

ALL-NBA PLAYERS

- Kawhi Leonard, Los Angeles Clippers
- Anthony Davis, Los Angeles Lakers
- James Harden, Houston Rockets
- Giannis Antetokounmpo, Milwaukee Bucks
- LeBron James, Los Angeles Lakers
- Damian Lillard, Portland Trail Blazers
- Luka Doncic, Dallas Mavericks
- Nikola Jokić, Denver Nuggets
- Rudy Gobert, Utah Jazz
- Khris Middleton, Milwaukee Bucks

- Bam Adebayo, Miami Heat
- Ben Simmons, Philadelphia 76ers
- Jayson Tatum, Boston Celtics
- Jimmy Butler, Miami Heat
- Russell Westbrook, Houston Rockets
- Chris Paul, Oklahoma City Thunder
- Donovan Mitchell, Utah Jazz
- Joel Embiid, Philadelphia 76ers
- Pascal Siakam, Toronto Raptors
- Trae Young, Atlanta Hawks

ALL-DEFENSIVE PLAYERS

- Ben Simmons, Philadelphia 76ers
- Marcus Smart, Boston Celtics
- Giannis Antetokounmpo, Milwaukee Bucks
- Anthony Davis, Los Angeles Lakers
- Rudy Gobert, Utah Jazz
- Eric Bledsoe, Milwaukee Bucks
- Kawhi Leonard, Los Angeles Clippers
- Kyle Lowry, Toronto Raptors
- Jayson Tatum, Boston Celtics
- Bam Adebayo, Miami Heat
- Patrick Beverly, Los Angeles Clippers
- Brook Lopez, Milwaukee Bucks
- P.J. Tucker, Houston Rockets
- Chris Paul, Oklahoma City Thunder
- Pascal Siakam, Toronto Raptors

CURRENT NBA DYNASTY SCORES (WORST TO FIRST)

30. Cleveland Cavaliers (7.125) (surprise, surprise)
29. New York Knicks (7.5)
28. Detroit Pistons (8.125)
27. San Antonio Spurs (8.25)
26. Minnesota Timberwolves (8.75)
25. Charlotte Hornets (8.75)
26. Brooklyn Nets (8.75) *score plummeted due to injuries to Kyrie Irving and Kevin Durant*
23. Golden State Warriors (9.125) *score plummeted due to injuries to Steph Curry and Klay Thompson*
22. Sacramento Kings (9.375)
21. Washington Wizards (9.375)
20. Atlanta Hawks (9.375)
19. Indiana Pacers (9.375) *score dipped due to injury to Victor Oladipo*
18. Orlando Magic (10)
17. Chicago Bulls (10.625)
16. Portland Trail Blazers (10.625)
15. Phoenix Suns (11.25)
14. Memphis Grizzlies (11.25)
13. Denver Nuggets (11.25)
12. Houston Rockets (11.875)
11. Dallas Mavericks (12.5)
10. Utah Jazz (13.75)
9. Philadelphia 76ers (16.25)
8. Oklahoma City Thunder (16.25)
7. New Orleans Pelicans (17.5)

TIED FOR #5: BOSTON CELTICS (18.125)

Of course, the last two teams had to tie and make me write an extra section. Oh well. Boston, baby. They've had lots of references in this book; they typically know what they're doing in terms of teambuilding. Danny Ainge has been a shrewd general manager, and his playing days with the Celtics qualified him as a Proven Winner. Jayson Tatum is an up-and-coming two-way megastar and the team has surrounded him with talent. Marcus Smart and Jaylen Brown are two hard-nosed defenders who don't need the ball as much. Kemba Walker was an All-Star and can be a dominator on the offensive end. Put all that together with a brilliant coach in Brad Stevens and you have all the elements of a potential dynasty.

TIED FOR #5: LOS ANGELES CLIPPERS (18.125)

The Clippers. Known for much of their existence as a dysfunctional little brother to the Lakers, LAC is finally building something of their own. Doc Rivers is a seasoned veteran coach and his previous stint in Boston qualified him for the "Proven Winner" category. Same goes for Kawhi Leonard, who won a title in both San Antonio and Toronto. Leonard is the linchpin of the team, the two-way wing who holds down the fort.

The Clippers have depth though; don't you think otherwise. Had Paul George not been dealing with a shoulder injury, there is a chance he could have been an All-Star, All-NBA, and All-Defensive Player (he earned all of those accolades the previous season). That change alone would have put the Clippers in the top three. Beyond that, Montrezl Harrell is at least a top-two contender for the 6MOY award. Patrick Beverly, Lou Williams, and Landry Shamet are all high-powered role players. The Clippers had the highest amount (four) of "high-level" role players in the league this season. The Clips have the stars, the coach, and the depth of a potential dynasty. Leonard and George's contracts expire after the next season, though. Better keep an eye on that.

#4: MIAMI HEAT (19.375)

The Heat are more of a Dark Horse than an actual contender this year. Most pundits would certainly put them below the Clippers, and I wouldn't necessarily disagree. That's not the point of this exercise, however. The Heat may not have two bona fide superstars like a lot of the top five teams do, but they don't need it (yet). What they do have is a cohesive unit that plays together and is led by a couple of fiery stars. Jimmy Butler and Bam(!) Adebayo are both slated to make All-NBA rosters. Adebayo is slated to make an All-Defense roster and is the apparent frontrunner for the MIP award.

The Heat have the most "Dynasty DNA" personnel (two) in the league. Pat Riley's coaching days with the Showtime Lakers qualified him for that category, and Andre Iguodala's (recent) time with the Warriors did the same. While the Heat don't have any role players that qualify as "high-level," they have eight players that qualify as "solid" role players. Nearly every player on the roster can make an open three, and almost all of them can play solid team defense. No one spots a championship window like Pat Riley; could this be the start of another run of titles for the Miami Heat?

#3: TORONTO RAPTORS (20.25)

I know, I was surprised too. While the Raptors are by no means a betting favorite to win the title this season, the narrative that they won the title last year simply because of Kawhi Leonard is dead in the ground. It is time we take this Toronto team much more seriously. Even without Leonard, the Raptors have seven returners from last year's title. Kyle Lowry may be nearing the end of his prime, but he is still slated to make an All-NBA team this year. Pascal Siakam has taken another unfathomable step in his progress after his MIP season last year. He is slated to make both an All-NBA team and an All-Defensive team.

Beyond them, the roster has plenty of seasoned veterans (like Marc Gasol and Serge Ibaka) mixed with up-and-comers (like OG Anunoby and Chris Boucher) who all have been productive this year. Nick Nurse has proven to be a top-five coach in this league, and he always knows how to bring the most out of his players. I'm not entirely sold on Siakam as a first option on a championship (let alone dynastic) team, but with the rising number of stars being traded and the fact that Masai Ujiri is still at the helm, I don't think Toronto is too worried.

#2: LOS ANGELES LAKERS (21.25)

Ah, the Lakers. The team with the most chapters in the book. Let's talk about them again, shall we? As I have eluded to in previous chapters, the Lakers are on the rise yet again. After a short but dreadful period of missing the playoffs, the Lakers have scored big on the market yet again. They signed LeBron (who you may recognize from the chapter named after him) and traded for All-NBA big man Anthony Davis. That's probably the best top two on any team in the league. They apparently found a good coach in the rejuvenated Frank Vogel. While his offensive sets are still a little lackluster, his defensive schemes have been good, and you don't necessarily need offensive sets while LBJ is around.

The Lakers don't have the depth of other contenders, but they have good role players. Danny Green won two titles in previous stints and is one of the better 3&D guys around. JaVale McGee also won two titles with the Golden State Dynasty. Rajon Rondo's best days may be behind him, but he still qualified as a Proven Winner for his time in Boston. The Lakers had the most (three) Proven Winners among the thirty teams (LeBron technically qualified as "Dynasty DNA"). The teams around LBJ typically have quick expiration dates, but this team is more than good enough to win two (if not more) titles in the near future.

#1: MILWAUKEE BUCKS (26.875)

Give me a second to explain before you guys really hurt my feelings. Is this the highest score out of any team in the book, let alone the thirty current teams? Yes. Is this the best team in the history of the NBA? Nope. This is where the "allowances" we gave in the introduction of this chapter come in to play. While Mike Budenholzer *probably* is not going to win COY, we have to cover our bases. The same goes for Brook Lopez making an All-Defense team. Note: Even if you take those two things away, the Bucks are still first out of thirty at 22.5. Yell at someone else.

Now that I have explained the score, let's look at the team. The Bucks had the best record in the league before it was stopped. Giannis Antetokounmpo probably is the MVP of the season, and he could easily win the DPOY as well. The Bucks have the most (three) players slated to make an All-Defense team. Coach Bud has implemented the perfect system for Antetokounmpo and his cohorts to thrive. Khris Middleton has erupted as a top fifteen player this season, further driving fear into the team's opponents. My biggest worry with this team is they have zero Proven Winners or Dynasty DNA. In fact, the Bucks' trip to the Conference Finals last season (2018–19) was the furthest a majority of the team had gone in the playoffs. I'd like to see a couple more guys on that roster who know how to play in the big moments. Antetokounmpo's contract situation is a looming shadow on this franchise (not as dire as the national media makes it seem, but until he signs the extension no one can be sure of anything). However, they have the MVP of the league with a potential decade of dominance still inside him. The Bucks have the best chance out of any team in the top five to become the NBA's next dynasty.

THE FINAL "FINAL THOUGHTS"

Seven(ish) decades. Seven dynasties. We've come a long way. Not only did we examine the dynasties of each era in the NBA, but we saw the league itself transform. We saw it progress from a league with fewer than ten teams, little to no non-white players, and no massive financial success, to this thirty-team behemoth with great players of all races and where five million dollars a year is considered a "cheap contract."

What sets the NBA apart from the other leagues (in my own opinion blah blah blah) is that there is a definite lineage. Not only are principles and play styles passed down from era to era, the people from those eras tend to stick around. Jerry West played in the '60s, coached in the '70s, and has been an executive since the '80s. He helped build the most recent dynasty in Golden State and has been the driving force in the Clippers' new era. Steve Kerr played for the Bulls dynasty, won two titles with the Spurs dynasty, and joined Jerry West in Golden State to coach the most recent dynasty. A lineage of success and winning in the NBA exists, which I just don't think we see in other American sports leagues.

The real reason for the "Dynasty DNA" category in the formula was to celebrate that lineage. Every dynasty following that of the Bulls had at least one member of a previous dynasty involved. Beyond that, the teams almost always had a coach who knew exactly how to use their players. You can win championships with zero chemistry and a couple of superstars. Hell, you can win them with perfect chemistry and no superstars (shout-out to 2004 Detroit). You just need to put all the pieces together to solve the Dynasty Puzzle.

If you guys made it this far, tweet "nice book nerd guy" @ aguibanezbaldor. Thank you very much for reading. :)

APPENDIX

CHAPTER 1: THE FIRST DYNASTY

Crowe, Jerry. "Minneapolis Sportswriter Helped Raise the Lakers." *Los Angeles Times*. April 27, 2009. https://www.latimes.com/archives/la-xpm-2009-apr-27-sp-crowe-nest27-story.html

Moore, Joe and Bontemps, Tim. "The ABA Is Long Gone, But it Remains the Soul of the NBA." *The Washington Post*. May 31, 2017. https://www.washingtonpost.com/graphics/sports/nba-aba-merger/?utm_term=.01e945c8b7ac

National Basketball Association. "Lakers Season Capsules." Lakers History. Accessed May 10, 2020. https://www.nba.com/lakers/history/seasoncapsule

Ripper, Joel. "John Kundla, Former Minneapolis Lakers Coach and Basketball Hall of Famer, Dies at 101." *Star Tribune*. July 24, 2017. https://www.startribune.com/john-kundla-former-minneapolis-lakers-coach-and-basketball-hall-of-famer-dies-at-101/436178233/

Schumacher, Michael. *Mr. Basketball: George Mikan, the Minneapolis Lakers, and the Birth of the NBA.* New York: Bloomsbury, 2007.

CHAPTER 2: DOMINANCE PERSONIFIED

Bird, Hayden. "How Red Auerbach Used the Ice Capades to Add Bill Russell to the Celtics' Best Draft Class." *Boston Globe.* June 22, 2016. https://www.boston.com/sports/boston-celtics/2016/06/22/bill-russell

Boon, Kyle. "Look: NBA Legend Bill Russell Takes a Knee with Presidential Medal of Freedom." *CBS Sports.* September 26, 2017. https://www.cbssports.com/nba/news/look-nba-legend-bill-russell-takes-a-knee-with-presidential-medal-of-freedom/

Dorsey, Jesse. "The Top Human Victory Cigars in the NBA." *Bleacher Report.* January 10, 2012. https://bleacherreport.com/articles/1017544-the-top-human-victory-cigars-in-the-nba

Forsberg, Chris. "How Tommy Heinsohn Was Nearly Mr. Caterpillar Instead of Mr. Celtics." *NBC Sports.* April 29, 2020. https://www.nbcsports.com/boston/celtics/how-tommy-heinsohn-was-nearly-mr-caterpillar-instead-mr-celtics

Hilton, Lisette. "Auerbach's Celtics Played as a Team." *ESPN.* Accessed May 10, 2020. http://www.espn.com/classic/biography/s/auerbach_red.html

Himmelsbach, Adam. "Why Was Boston Garden Nearly Empty When Bill Russell's Number Was Retired in 1972?" *Boston*

Globe. October 17, 2017. https://www.bostonglobe.com/sports/
celtics/2017/10/07/why-was-boston-garden-nearly-empty-
when-bill-russell-number-was-retired/f2hGuHb1tEJiirpOO-
BeqcP/story.html

Reed, Tom. "Defiance, Bragging: A History of Victory Cigars, from
Red to MJ, Team Canada's Party, Buckeyes and Bama, LeBron
and Steph." *The Athletic*. March 20, 2019. https://theathletic.
com/871974/2019/03/20/smell-of-success-a-history-of-victory-
cigars-from-red-to-mj-team-canadas-party-buckeyes-and-ba-
ma-lebron-and-steph/?redirected=1

Rohrbach, Ben. "Whose NBA Career Is Better? Stephen Curry vs.
Jerry West." *Yahoo! Sports*. June 4, 2020. https://sports.yahoo.
com/whose-nba-career-is-better-stephen-curry-vs-jerry-
west-144914742.html

Schwartz, Larry. "Celtics Tried to Pass on Ultimate Passer." *ESPN*.
Accessed May 10, 2020. https://www.espn.com/sportscentury/
features/00014144.html

Simmons, Bill. "Mr. Russell's House." Filmed February 2013 in
Seattle, WA. NBA TV Originals, 13:05. https://www.nba.
com/video/channels/originals/2013/02/07/20130207-rus-
sell-house-excerpt.nba

Sports Reference LLC. "K.C. Jones Coaches Index." Basketball
Reference. Accessed May 10, 2020. https://www.basketball-ref-
erence.com/coaches/joneskc01c.html

Turner Sports Network. "Bill Russell Biography." NBA Encyclopedia. Accessed May 10, 2020. http://archive.nba.com/history/players/russell_bio.html

FOREWORD TO PART 2

Myers, Daniel. "About Box Plus/Minus (BPM)." *Basketball Reference.* February 2020. https://www.basketball-reference.com/about/bpm2.html#:~:text=Box%20Plus%2FMinus%2C%20Version%202.0,player%20is%20on%20the%20court.&text=A%20value%20of%20%2B5.0%20means,average%20production%20from%20another%20player.

CHAPTER 3: THE SHOWTIME LAKERS

Abdul-Jabbar, Kareem. "What My Life in Sports Has Taught Me." *Thought Economics.* July 17, 2019. https://thoughteconomics.com/kareem-abdul-jabbar/

AP. "Lakers Drop Westhead as Coach." *The New York Times.* November 20, 1981. https://www.nytimes.com/1981/11/20/sports/lakers-drop-westhead-as-coach.html

Aschburner, Steve. "Larry Bird, Magic Johnson Lifted the NBA with Heated Rivalry." *NBA.* December 28, 2019. https://www.nba.com/article/2019/12/28/magic-johnson-larry-bird-rivalry-40th-anniversary

Bonk, Thomas. "June 16, 1975: A Banner Day for Lakers." *Los Angeles Times*. December 25, 1987. https://www.latimes.com/archives/la-xpm-1987-12-25-sp-21142-story.html

Cobbs, Chris. "The Punch: Tomjanovich and Washington Both Still Feel the Pain from That Terrible Moment." *Los Angeles Times*. January 28, 1985. https://www.latimes.com/archives/la-xpm-1985-01-28-sp-10262-story.html

Elliott, Helene. "Jack McKinney's Bike Ride Changed Lakers' History." *Los Angeles Times*. February 9, 2012. https://www.latimes.com/sports/la-xpm-2012-feb-09-la-sp-lakers-mckinney-20120210-story.html

Hartwell, Darren. "This Date in Celtics History: C's Crush Lakers in 'Memorial Day Massacre.'" *NBC SPORTS*. May 27, 2020. https://www.nbcsports.com/boston/celtics/date-celtics-history-cs-crush-lakers-memorial-day-massacre

Hojnacki, Seth. "Photo Timeline of Storied LA Lakers-Boston Celtics Rivalry." *Bleacher Report*. February 20, 2013. https://bleacherreport.com/articles/1536767-photo-timeline-of-storied-la-lakers-boston-celtics-rivalry

Johnson, Earvin "Magic." *My Life*. New York: Fawcett Books, 1992.

Montgomery, Paul L. "Abdul-Jabbar Fined $5,000 for One Punch." *The New York Times*. October 21, 1977. https://www.nytimes.com/1977/10/21/archives/abduljabbar-fined-5000-for-one-punch-punch-brings-abduljabbar-5000.html

Palsey, James. "How Cheerleading Evolved from One Man Yelling in Minnesota to 4.5 Million Leaping Cheerleaders." *Business Insider*. January 31, 2020. https://www.businessinsider.com/ evolution-of-cheerleading-in-photos-2020-1

Politi, Steve. "Who Knows What Nets Could Have Been If Dr. J Stayed?" *NJ.com*. March 30, 2019. https://www.nj.com/ nets/2012/04/politi_who_knows_what_nets_cou.html

Pumerantz, Zack. "The 50 Best Trash Talk Lines in Sports History." *Bleacher Report*. June 29, 2012. https://bleacherreport.com/ articles/1238737-the-50-best-trash-talk-lines-in-sports-history

Schilken, Chuck. "NBA Journeyman Luke Ridnour Is Traded to His Fifth Team in Six Days." *Los Angeles Times*. June 30, 2015. https://www.latimes.com/sports/sportsnow/la-sp-sn-luke-rid-nour-nba-trades-20150630-story.html

Schmid, John. "Milwaukee's Trauma Care Initiatives Are Meant to Heal. Now They Are at the Heart of the City's Racial Divide." *Milwaukee Journal Sentinel*. June 18, 2019. https:// www.jsonline.com/story/news/solutions/2019/06/18/centu-ries-old-racism-haunts-efforts-treat-milwaukee-trauma-epi-demic/2580146002/

Trucks, Rob. "Why I Thought About Killing My NBA Head Coach (and Why I Didn't Do it)." *Deadspin*. March 14, 2014. https:// deadspin.com/why-i-thought-about-murdering-my-nba-coach-and-why-i-d-1537818035

Walker, Rhiannon. "The Day Magic Johnson Stepped in at Center and Dropped 42 Points on Philly." *The Undefeated*. May 16,

2018. https://theundefeated.com/features/the-day-magic-johnson-stepped-in-at-center-and-dropped-42-points-on-philly/

CHAPTER 4: HIS ROYAL AIRNESS AND THE CHICAGO BULLS DYNASTY

Adande, J.A. "Michael Jordan's Famous 'I'm back' Fax, 25 Years Later." *ESPN.* March 18, 2020. https://www.espn.com/nba/story/_/id/12501628/michael-jordan-famous-back-fax-25-years-later

Barry, Dan. "The Triangle Offense, a Simple Yet Perplexing System, Dies." *The New York Times.* June 28, 2017. https://www.nytimes.com/2017/06/28/sports/basketball/triangle-offense-new-york-knicks.html

Fernandez, Gabriel. "How the Legend of Michael Jordan's 'flu game' Has Evolved Since the 1997 NBA Finals." *CBS Sports.* May 20, 2020. https://www.cbssports.com/nba/news/how-the-legend-of-michael-jordans-flu-game-has-evolved-since-the-1997-nba-finals/

Gano, Rick. "Bulls Acquire Rodman from Spurs." *The Washington Post.* October 3, 1995. https://www.washingtonpost.com/archive/sports/1995/10/03/bulls-acquire-rodman-from-spurs/05ef2039-04da-4483-a7bd-84219c40417d/

NBA.com Staff. "Legends Profile: Michael Jordan." *NBA History.* Accessed June 4, 2020. https://www.nba.com/history/legends/profiles/michael-jordan

Owens, Jason. "Craig Ehlo 'shocked' by Ron Harper's 'Last Dance' Comments, Doesn't Remember Him 'wanting to play defense'." *Yahoo! Sports.* April 30, 2020. https://sports.yahoo.com/craig-ehlo-shocked-by-ron-harpers-last-dance-comments-i-dont-remember-him-wanting-to-play-defense-185955447.html

Washington Post. "Excerpts of Jordan's Remarks." Accessed June 5, 2020. https://www.washingtonpost.com/archive/sports/1993/10/07/excerpts-of-jordans-remarks/6fb507f6-7692-4161-b959-a7d8b2c39aff/

Wise, Mike. "N.B.A. Preview '97-'98: End of Line for Dynasty? Aging Bulls to Face Challenge from Several Teams." *The New York Times.* October 29, 1997. https://www.nytimes.com/1997/10/29/sports/nba-preview-97-98-end-line-for-dynasty-aging-bulls-face-challenge-several-teams.html

Zillgitt, Jeff. "'The Last Dance': How the Pistons Employed 'The Jordan Rules' Against Michael Jordan." *USA Today.* April 27, 2020. https://www.usatoday.com/story/sports/nba/bulls/2020/04/27/the-last-dance-revisiting-the-jordan-rules-used-pistons/3032835001/

CHAPTER 5: THE SECOND COMING OF SHOWTIME

Bucher, Ric. "An Oral History of the 2003-04 Los Angeles Lakers, the 1st Super Team." *Bleacher Report.* May 26, 2015. https://bleacherreport.com/articles/2468658-an-oral-history-of-the-2003-2004-los-angeles-lakers-the-first-super-team

Ding, Kevin. "Kobe Bryant's Predraft Workout Has Become Stuff of Lakers, and NBA, Legend." *Bleacher Report.* June 24, 2014. https://bleacherreport.com/articles/2108226-kobe-bryants-predraft-workout-has-become-stuff-of-lakers-and-nba-legend

Draper, Kevin. "Kobe Bryant and the Sexual Assault Case That Was Dropped but Not Forgotten." *The New York Times.* January 27, 2020. https://www.nytimes.com/2020/01/27/sports/basketball/kobe-bryant-rape-case.html

Farrell, Perry A. *Tales from the Detroit Pistons Locker Room.* Illinois: Sports Publishing LLC, 2004.

Golianopoulos, Thomas. ""An Unmitigated Disaster": An Oral History of the Lockout-Shortened 1999 NBA Season." *The Ringer.* February 19, 2019. https://www.theringer.com/nba/2019/2/19/18228706/lockout-1999-season-san-antonio-spurs-new-york-knicks

Lazenby, Roland. *Showboat: The Life of Kobe Bryant.* New York: Back Bay Books, 2016.

"Pro Basketball; Tension Between O'Neal and Bryant Is Rising Every Day." *The New York Times.* January 11, 2001. https://www.nytimes.com/2001/01/11/sports/pro-basketball-tension-between-o-neal-and-bryant-is-rising-every-day.html?pagewanted=1

Sheridan, Chris. "2002 Lakers-Kings Game 6 at Heart of Donaghy Allegations." *ESPN.* June 10, 2008. https://www.espn.com/nba/news/story?id=3436401

CHAPTER 6: THE BIG FUNDAMENTAL AND HIS SPURS

Back, Ethan. "Tim Duncan: The San Antonio Spurs Superstar Will Never Get the Props He Deserves." *Bleacher Report*. January 22, 2011. https://bleacherreport.com/articles/574564-tim-duncan-the-san-antonio-spurs-superstar-will-never-get-the-props-deserved

McCallum, Jack. "The Big Fundamental to Prevail in the Championship Series, the Nets Will Have to Exploit Flaws in the Game of Spurs Star Tim Duncan—If They Can Find Any." *Sports Illustrated*. June 9, 2003. https://vault.si.com/vault/2003/06/09/703061-toc

NBA.com Staff. "Top Moments: Twin Towers Ride Off to Sunset with Another Title." *NBA History*. Accessed June 4, 2020. https://www.nba.com/history/top-moments/2003-spurs-championship-duncan-robinson

Quinn, Sam. "2020 NBA Buyout Market: How Midseason Free Agency Works, and Who Could Be Available After the Trade Deadline." *CBS Sports*. February 26, 2020. https://www.cbssports.com/nba/news/2020-nba-buyout-market-how-midseason-free-agency-works-and-who-could-be-available-after-the-trade-deadline/#:~:text=How%20do%20buyouts%20work%3F,team%20as%20a%20free%20agent.

Stein, Marc. "NBA Suspends Stoudemire, Diaw for Leaving Bench." *ESPN*. May 15, 2007. https://www.espn.com/nba/playoffs2007/news/story?id=2871615

Ziller, Tom. "A Complete Primer on Drafting International NBA Prospects." *SBNATION*. June 25, 2014. https://www.sbnation. com/nba/2014/6/25/5820488/nba-draft-2014-international-prospects-dante-exum-dario-saric

CHAPTER 7: THE GOLDEN STATE DYNASTY

Bieler, Des. "Steph Curry Fined $50,000 for Throwing Mouthpiece Toward Referee but Avoids Suspension." *The Washington Post*. October 23, 2017. https://www.washingtonpost.com/news/early-lead/wp/2017/10/23/steph-curry-fined-50000-for-throwing-mouthpiece-toward-referee-but-avoids-suspension/

Conway, Tyler. "Mark Jackson Fired by Warriors: Latest Details, Comments and Reaction." *Bleacher Report*. May 6, 2014. https:// bleacherreport.com/articles/2051681-mark-jackson-reportedly-fired-by-warriors-latest-details-comments-and-reaction

Evans, Kelly. "Charles Barkley Doesn't Respect Kevin Durant's Decision." *The Undefeated*. July 6, 2016. https://theundefeated. com/features/charles-barkley-doesnt-respect-kevin-durants-decision/

Golliver, Ben. "George Karl Rips Mark Jackson's 'bush' Tactics, identifies Andre Iguodala as 'mole.'" *Sports Illustrated*. November 29, 2013. https://www.si.com/nba/2013/11/29/george-karl-rips-mark-jackson-andre-iguodala-mole

Golliver, Ben. "NBA Announces Record Salary Cap for 2016-17 After Historic Climb." *Sports Illustrated*. July 2, 2016. https://

www.si.com/nba/2016/07/03/nba-salary-cap-record-numbers-2016-adam-silver

Haynes, Chris. "Sources: Draymond Green Suspended After Calling Kevin Durant a 'bitch'." *Yahoo! Sports*. November 13, 2018. https://sports.yahoo.com/sources-warriors-expected-sit-draymond-green-confrontation-kevin-durant-223801633.html

Howard-Cooper, Scott. "On the Clock: Q&A with Former Golden State Warriors GM Larry Riley." *NBA*. June 8, 2017. https://www.nba.com/article/2017/06/08/clock-larry-riley-golden-state-warriors-drafting-stephen-curry-2009

Jenkins, Lee. "The Birth of the Warriors' Death Lineup." *Sports Illustrated*. June 7, 2016. https://www.si.com/nba/2016/06/07/golden-state-warriors-death-lineup-nba-finals-cleveland-cavaliers

Mahoney, Rob. "Fine Tuning: Coaching Stephen Curry, Best Shooter in the Universe." *Sports Illustrated*. April 7, 2015. https://www.si.com/nba/2015/04/07/stephen-curry-steve-kerr-warriors-coaching-staff-bruce-fraser

Rapp, Timothy. "Andrew Wiggins, Timberwolves Agree to 5-Year, $146.5 Million Contract Extension." *Bleacher Report*. October 11, 2017. https://bleacherreport.com/articles/2722896-andrew-wiggins-timberwolves-agree-to-5-year-148-million-contract-extension

CHAPTER 8: BIRD'S CELTICS

Boren, Cindy. "Remembering Len Bias 30 Years After His Death: 'He was It.'" *The Washington Post*. June 19, 2016. https://www. washingtonpost.com/news/early-lead/wp/2016/06/19/remembering-len-bias-30-years-after-his-death-he-was-it/

Mckenna, Henry. "Bill Walton Tells the Story of How He Ended up with the Celtics." *Boston.com*. March 28, 2016. https://www. boston.com/sports/boston-celtics/2016/03/28/566069

Reichert, Chirs. "The Original "Draft and Stash" Player." *Fansided*. 2017. https://fansided.com/2016/06/14/nba-draft-larry-bird-boston-celtics/

Shapiro, Leonard. "Red Auerbach." *The Washington Post*. May 10, 1981. https://www.washingtonpost.com/archive/sports/1981/05/10/red-auerbach/48669cd3-b026-4865-a9d3-c3d2e3f539dd/

CHAPTER 9: LEBRON'S LEGACY

Axson, Scooby. "Ray Allen Not Invited to '08 Celtics Championship Reunion." *Sports Illustrated*. March 20, 2017. https://www. si.com/nba/2017/03/20/celtics-reunion-ray-allen-not-invited

Beck, Howard. "N.B.A. Reaches a Tentative Deal to Save the Season." *The New York Times*. November 26, 2011. https://www. nytimes.com/2011/11/27/sports/basketball/nba-and-basketball-players-reach-deal-to-end-lockout.html

Deb, Sopan. "LeBron James Faces Backlash Unseen Since 'The Decision.'" *The New York Times*. October 15, 2019. https://www.nytimes.com/2019/10/15/sports/basketball/lebron-china-burned-jerseys.html

Harper, Zach. "LeBron James After Winning the 2016 NBA Finals: 'Cleveland, this is for you!'." *CBS Sports*. June 19, 2016. https://www.cbssports.com/nba/news/lebron-james-after-winning-the-2016-nba-finals-cleveland-this-is-for-you/

McMenamin, Dave. "When LeBron Swooped in and Changed the Course of Cavs' History." *ESPN*. June 27, 2016. https://www.espn.com/nba/playoffs/2016/story/_/id/16544563/nba-finals-2016-oral-history-lebron-chasedown-block

Zucker, Joseph. "LeBron James Says He Felt Dan Gilbert's Letter When He Left Cavs Was Racial." *Bleacher Report*. October 17, 2017. https://bleacherreport.com/articles/2739194-lebron-james-says-he-felt-dan-gilberts-letter-when-he-left-cavs-was-racial

CHAPTER 10: THE DYNASTY THAT NEVER WAS

Golliver, Ben. "Grade the Trade: Thunder Trade James Harden to Rockets." *Sports Illustrated*. October 28, 2012. https://www.si.com/nba/2012/10/28/james-harden-trade-thunder-rockets

Spears, Marc J. "The KD Question: Did Kevin Durant Play His Last Game for the Thunder?" *The Undefeated*. May 31, 2016. https://theundefeated.com/features/the-kd-question-did-kevin-durant-play-his-last-game-for-the-thunder/

CONCLUSION

Stein, Marc. "N.B.A. Owners Set a July 31 Restart, All in Florida." *The New York Times.* June 4, 2020. https://www.nytimes.com/2020/06/04/sports/basketball/coronavirus-nba-disney-world-restart.html

Woike, Dan. "NBA Suspends Season Indefinitely Over Coronavirus Pandemic." *Los Angeles Times.* March 11, 2020. https://www.latimes.com/sports/story/2020-03-11/nba-suspends-season-indefinitely-over-coronavirus-pandemic